D0073336

William Styron Revisited

Twayne's United States Authors Series

Warren French, Editor
University College of Swansea, Wales

TUSAS 577

WILLIAM STYRON
Photograph © 1982 Stathis Orphanos.

William Styron Revisited

Samuel Coale

Wheaton College

Twayne Publishers • Boston
A Division of G. K. Hall & Co.

William Styron Revisited
Samuel Coale

Copyright 1991 by G. K. Hall & Co.
All rights reserved.
Published by Twayne Publishers
A division of G. K. Hall & Co.
70 Lincoln Street
Boston, Massachusetts 02111

Copyediting supervised by India Koopman.
Book production by Janet Z. Reynolds.
Book design by Barbara Anderson.
Typeset by Compositors Corp., Cedar Rapids, Iowa.

First published 1991.
10 9 8 7 6 5 4 3 2 1

Library of Congress Cataloging-in-Publication Data

Coale, Samuel.
    William Styron revisited / Samuel Coale.
        p.   cm. — (Twayne's United States authors series ; TUSAS 577)
    Includes bibliographical references (p.   ) and index.
    ISBN 0-8057-7619-2
    1. Styron, William, 1925–   —Criticism and interpretation.
    I. Title.   II. Series.
    PS3569.T9Z624   1991
    813'.54—dc20   90-21108

66885

To Gray and Sam
"Consider hope! Consider joy!"

Contents

Publisher's Note

William Styron Revisited by Samuel Coale is a timely retrospective of Styron's literary career and takes account of the numerous important works written by Styron since 1973, when Twayne Publishers issued *William Styron* by Marc Ratner. We are pleased to offer this new evaluation of Styron's achievement.

Preface

So much has been written over the years about William Styron and his work that it becomes very difficult to approach them from new perspectives. Critics seem evenly divided between his strengths and his weaknesses, and no final judgment is yet in. This is, perhaps, as it should be, since Styron is very much alive and continuing to work.

I decided on two important points. One deals with the clinical depression, for which Styron was hospitalized in 1985–86, in an attempt to conjure up a general psychological and/or metaphysical portrait of the author at this writing. The other involves examining in detail the various critical lenses through which Styron has been observed over the years. The latter includes his position as a southern writer, as a Gothic romancer in the American romance tradition, and as an American existentialist of the fifties. Each of these perspectives was valid in its own time, but each seems finally lacking in trying to get to the heart of the matter.

It seems to me that at the center of Styron's fiction lurks what I've chosen to call the encapsulated self. This is a "fiction" about the self that appears to be essentially asocial, narcissistic, self-regarding, and at times claustrophobically caged. Such a self may possibly be more a symptom of our times since World War II than a diagnosis or vision of those times. And such a self remains mired in its own confused and confusing notions of guilt, evil, responsibility, and anxiety.

Many writers since World War II—Bellow, Updike, Didion, and Mailer, to name just a few—have created novels that are at once critical of and implicated in the social order that surrounds them. It is as if they cannot function unless they acknowledge both their dependency on society and their desire to be independent from it, an outlook not necessarily foreign to any good novelist but particularly uneasy in its simultaneous attraction to and repulsion from social contexts. This aspect may, finally, be the uncertain center of most good American fiction.

Styron's fiction seems most successful when he is able to link the self at the center of it—Nat Turner, Stingo, Sophie Zawistowska—to a wider pattern or event, either to historical incidents or, in the case of *The Long March,* to a ready-made system like the military. Such "anchors" provide an outlet or connection for essentially meditative, introspective characters who tend to sink too often into their own meditations and who, if not careful, cannot escape from them.

Many problems in Styron's work continue to surface. He often confuses a character's Christian beliefs in a historical context with his own desire to use such beliefs as a pattern and structure for his novels. This practice often results in an inconclusive confrontation between an unstable, meaningless universe and a self-diagnosed, old-fashioned Christian pattern of resurrection and redemption grafted upon that universe. At times the carefully shaped architecture of the novels clashes with the irremediable sufferings in them.

In a similar context, Styron often ends his novels in an upbeat manner, an ending that raises questions about the depth and understanding of the narrator's experiences and at times undercuts the more tragic visions of the story. The upshot suggests a kind of uncertain blur, an out-of-focus perspective that raises as many questions as it tries to answer.

Having interviewed and corresponded with Styron in 1969 for my dissertation at Brown University on southern writers, I have based much of my own perspective on the author and his work from that time. As with any ongoing process, I hope that this book suggests as much as it tries to define and leaves the continuing exploration of Styron's fiction open and filled with possibilities.

This book concentrates primarily on *The Confessions of Nat Turner* and *Sophie's Choice* and views Styron's earlier fictions as preludes to these two novels. In particular, *Sophie's Choice* stands as the triumph of his art, and it is toward this conclusion that I have directed this book. No understanding of contemporary America's moods and uncertainties can be complete, I think, without taking Styron's fiction into account, and his novels, particularly his last two, both celebrate and transcend their eras. It is a tribute to him and his art that one more critical exploration of his work has appeared.

Samuel Coale

Wheaton College

Acknowledgments

I would like to thank Random House and Bantam Books for permission to use copyright material and quote from William Styron's novels and collected essays.

William Styron was the first novelist I ever interviewed, when I was working on my dissertation at Brown University in 1969. I am extremely grateful for our relationship and his assistance over these last two decades and hope that such a long-standing friendship will continue. None of this, of course, would be possible without the care and careful assistance of editors and friends Warren French and Liz Fowler; Roberta Winston, who edited the manuscript; and Janet Reynolds, who supervised its production. The acceptance and publication of my second book for Twayne has been a very cheerful process.

There are several other people I wish to thank, many of whom I met and discussed Styron's fiction with at the Seventh Winthrop Symposium on Major Modern Writers at Winthrop College in Rock Hill, South Carolina, 9–12 April 1986: Jackson R. Bryer and Melvin J. Friedman, who revived my interest in Styron and accepted my article on his work for *Papers on Language and Literature* (1987), and several other Styron critics, including John Kenny Crane, Daniel W. Ross, Eva B. Mills, Earl J. Wilcox, and Rhoda Sirlin.

The continued support of Wheaton College for my scholarship cannot go unnoticed and should be celebrated.

Finally, there are two people—and a dog—without whom none of this would have been written. To my wife, Gray, who puts up with my obsessions and strivings for revelation; to my son Sam, who puts all things in perspective and good-naturedly brings me down to earth; and to Mavro, the black lab, who shares long days in my study without complaint: to these three, I am deeply indebted.

Chronology

1925 William Styron born 11 June in Newport News, Virginia.

1939 Mother, Pauline Abraham Styron, dies.

1940 Sent to Christchurch School near Urbana, Virginia.

1942 Enrolls at Davidson College, Davidson, North Carolina.

1943 Enlists in the Marine Corps and transfers to Duke University in Durham, North Carolina. Studies with William Blackburn.

1945 Discharged from the marines as a second lieutenant.

1947 Graduates from Duke University with a B.A. Becomes associate editor at McGraw-Hill in New York. Studies with Hiram Haydn at the New School for Social Research.

1949 Lives in a boardinghouse in the Flatbush section of Brooklyn, New York.

1951 *Lie Down in Darkness.* Called up by the marines for Korea.

1952 Prix de Rome Fellowship in Rome. Helps found the *Paris Review.*

1953 "Long March" in *Discovery.* Marries Rose Burgunder in Rome on 4 May.

1954 Moves to Roxbury, Connecticut.

1955 Daughter Susanna born.

1958 Daughter Paola born.

1959 Son Tom born.

1960 *Set This House on Fire.*

1964 Teaching fellow at Silliman College, Yale University.

1966 Member of the National Institute of Arts and Letters. Lectures in Egypt with Robert Penn Warren. Daughter Alexandra born.

1967 *The Confessions of Nat Turner.* Awarded Pulitzer Prize.

1968 Delegate to Democratic National Convention. Receives honorary degrees from Duke, Tufts, and Wilberforce universities and the New School for Social Research in New York.

1969 Witness at trial of the "Chicago Seven."

1970   Awarded Howells Medal of Fiction, American Academy of Arts and Letters.

1971   "Marriott, the Marine" in *Esquire*.

1972   *In the Clap Shack* produced at Yale Repertory Company.

1973   *In the Clap Shack.*

1977   Attends Moscow conference of American and Soviet writers.

1978   Father, William Clark Styron, dies.

1980   *Sophie's Choice.* Receives the first American Book Award for fiction.

1981   Delivers commencement address at Duke.

1982   *This Quiet Dust and Other Writings.* Film version of *Sophie's Choice* opens to rave reviews. Presents National Medal for Literature to John Cheever.

1985   "Love Day" in *Esquire*. Hospitalized for clinical depression.

1987   Elected to the American Academy of Arts and Letters. Invited to the Soviet embassy to meet Mikhail Gorbachev.

1988   "A Tidewater Morning" in *Esquire*. Receives the MacDowell Medal. Announcement of filming of *Lie Down in Darkness,* with Styron as coproducer.

1989   At work on *The Way of the Warrior.* "Darkness Visible" in *Vanity Fair.*

1990   *Darkness Visible: A Memoir of Madness.*

Chapter One

William Styron:
A Polarized Soul

By now the literary and biographical accomplishments and most of the details of William Styron's career and life are well known. A quick overview can root that life in its particularities, after which we can explore in greater detail those events and people which seem to have influenced the man the most. Styron was born in Newport News, Virginia, on 11 June 1925. He attended Davidson College in Davidson, North Carolina, in 1942; enlisted in the U.S. Marines; and through the navy's V-12 program, transferred to Duke University in Durham. Under the tutelage of writing professor William Blackburn, he came to appreciate Elizabethan and seventeenth-century English prose, as well as the orotund and rhetorical flourishes of Thomas Wolfe, and wrote stories for the *Archive,* Duke's literary magazine.

Late in 1944 Styron was sent to Parris Island, and in May 1945, after completing Officer Candidate School at Camp Lejeune, he was commissioned a second lieutenant at Quantico. An infamous episode marked his military career at Camp Lejeune when, suffering from a case of trench mouth, he was put into a venereal disease ward for four and a half months. (His only play, *In the Clap Shack,* which was produced by the Yale Repertory Company in December 1972, was based on this incident.) From Quantico he was sent to serve as a guard at the Naval Disciplinary Barracks on Hart's Island in New York Harbor and was discharged, without having seen combat, in late 1945.

Styron knew early on that he wanted to be a writer. After the war he set himself the task of writing a first novel. He returned to Duke in March 1946, sailed to and from Trieste on a cattle boat as an assistant veterinarian in the summer of 1946, and attended the Bread Loaf Writers' Conference in Middlebury, Vermont. He received his B.A. from Duke in March 1947, barely missing out on a Rhodes scholarship—he had failed physics four times—and wound up as an associate editor in the trade book division of McGraw-Hill in New York, reading through the "slush pile" of incoming manuscripts.

Professor Blackburn suggested that Styron take a creative writing course with Hiram Haydn at the New School for Social Research in New York, and he did. Haydn was the famous novelist and teacher who later became an editor for Bobbs-Merrill and Random House and who helped found Atheneum Publishers in 1959. In October 1947 Styron was fired by Thomas Wolfe's last editor at McGraw-Hill and, so as to be able to write full-time, accepted the financial support of his father and a small inheritance from his grandmother. He wrote in New York, in Durham, and in a Flatbush boardinghouse in Brooklyn in the spring of 1949, and wound up at the home of Sigrid de Lima and her mother—an author and the publicity director of the New School, respectively—at Valley College in Nyack, New York, until May 1950, when he returned to New York. Writer's block often haunted his efforts, but he persisted.

Early in 1951 Styron was called up by the marines for the war in Korea, but Hiram Haydn managed to postpone his going until he could finish Peyton Loftis's famous monologue at the end of *Lie Down in Darkness*, a task Styron completed in less than three weeks, losing fifteen pounds in the process. He then returned to Camp Lejeune as a member of the Second Marine Division and was finally discharged, in late summer, because of a congenital cataract.

On 10 September 1951 Bobbs-Merrill published *Lie Down in Darkness*, and in less than a month it had sold twenty thousand copies and been welcomed by rave reviews. Styron was an "overnight" success at the age of twenty-six. The result was the Prix de Rome Fellowship of the American Academy of Arts and Letters, which included a stipend of three thousand dollars and a year's room and board at the American Academy in Rome. On the way to Rome, after having toured England and Denmark, he stopped in Paris where he met such fellow writers as George Plimpton, Peter Matthiessen, and Donald Hall and helped found the *Paris Review*. While there he also wrote, in June and July of 1952, what would become *The Long March*, then entitled "Like Prisoners Waking"; the work was published in the journal *discovery* as "Long March" in February 1953 and in book form as a Modern Library paperback edition in October 1956.

In October 1952 Styron at last arrived in Rome. There, in 1953, the literary critic and writing professor, Louis D. Rubin, formally introduced him to Rose Burgunder, a member of a wealthy and socially prominent Jewish family in Baltimore. Burgunder, who had received her M.A. in aesthetics at Johns Hopkins the previous year and had met Styron there briefly when he had come to lecture, was in Rome on a poetry fellowship. (She has since gone on to publish books of poetry, including *Summer to Summer* [1965] and *Thieves' Afternoon* [1973]). On their first date, at the bar of the Excelsior Hotel, Styron and Burgunder were accompanied by Truman Capote; for their wedding, on 4 May 1953, the novelist Irwin Shaw served as host.

From Rome the newly married Styrons traveled to Ravello, where he visited the set of John Huston's film *Beat the Devil* and began not only *Set This House on Fire* but also a novella about a prison guard, a part of which surfaced and was published in 1987 as "Blankenship" in the academic journal *Papers on Language and Literature.* By October 1954 the Styrons had settled in Roxbury, Connecticut—where they still live, though they have also acquired a house on Martha's Vineyard—and he set to work in earnest on *Set This House on Fire.*

Books, children, and honors followed. *Set This House on Fire* was published by Random House on the Styrons' seventh wedding anniversary, 4 May 1960, to tepid and negative American reviews that seriously undercut his early literary success. *The Confessions of Nat Turner,* published by Random House, appeared on 9 October 1967 and was greeted by rave reviews—before the assault by black critics on Styron's integrity as a writer. Fifty thousand words were excerpted in *Harper's,* for which Styron received what at the time was the highest price ever paid to a writer publishing in that magazine. The novel went on to win the Pulitzer Prize in fiction. On 11 June 1979, Styron's fifty-fourth birthday, Random House published *Sophie's Choice,* which remained on the *New York Times* best-seller list for forty-seven weeks and won the first American Book Award for fiction in 1980.

During this period the Styrons had four children: Susanna, born in 1955; Paola, in 1958; Tom, in 1959; and Alexandra, in 1966. Also during this time Styron spoke out on such issues as capital punishment, racism, Vietnam and political persecution of writers, and supported the 1968 presidential candidacy of Eugene McCarthy. Styron became a teaching fellow at Silliman College at Yale in 1964, was elected a member of the National Institute of Arts and Letters in 1966, and received honorary degrees from Duke, the New School, Tufts University, and Wilberforce University in 1968. And in 1970 the American Academy of Arts and Letters awarded him the Howells Medal for the best work in fiction over a five-year period.

In more recent years Styron has attended the Moscow conference of American and Soviet writers (1977), given the commencement address at Duke (1981), published his essays as *This Quiet Dust* (1982), and received the MacDowell Medal (1988). With other selected American authors, he was invited to meet Mikhail Gorbachev at the Soviet embassy on 8 December 1987, and on 10 December of that year he was elected to the American Academy of Arts and Letters. The 1982 film based on *Sophie's Choice* was a critical triumph and won the Academy Award for actress Meryl Streep the following spring. As of this writing, Jay H. Fuchs, a theatrical producer, is working on a film production of *Lie Down in Darkness,* with Styron serving as coproducer.

The Darkness of Depression

The sense of a relatively placid existence, one that had produced a literary achievement based on a solid critical and popular reputation, was shattered in the late 1980s when Styron publicly disclosed his hospitalization for clinical depression. He made this disclosure in an editorial in the *New York Times* on 19 December 1988, following an in-depth interview with fellow writer and marine Philip Caputo in *Esquire* in December 1986, and in his confessional article, "Darkness Visible," in *Vanity Fair* in December 1989. The article was expanded and published as a book, *Darkness Visible: A Memoir of Madness,* in September, 1990 by Random House. The *Times* article "brought the most response of anything I have ever written,"[1] Styron explained. He had been admitted to the psychiatric ward of Yale–New Haven Hospital on 14 December 1985, been released on 2 February 1986, and begun attending Alcoholics Anonymous meetings.

The experience had been devastating. "A palpable shroud of melancholy descends on you and becomes a pain as severe as a crushed knee," Styron told Caputo. "You cannot bear living any longer. . . . You lose your self-esteem. You tell yourself, 'I'm not worthy to be pulled out of this. Everything I have ever done is a bloated monstrosity of my ego, and I have committed atrocities against my fellow man that are unpardonable.' You feel guilty for everything you've done."[2] Styron explained that he had experienced "a kind of biochemical meltdown. . . . The sick brain plays evil tricks on its inhabiting spirit. . . . The smallest commonplace of domestic life . . . lacerates like a blade. [Such] depression comes to resemble physical anguish . . . there is no respite at all . . . suicide [seems like an act] of blind necessity."[3] Another victim of such depression described a similar state: "As an apostate Roman Catholic with a dark streak of Polish romanticism, I had always felt guilty about *something.*" He too was overcome with "the corrosive sense of worthlessness and pessimism. . . . I cried . . . seeing Meryl Streep in 'Sophie's Choice.' "[4]

That same victim also described his depression as "the one major experience I have in common with Dostoyevsky, Poe, Hawthorne," a notion similar to Styron's: "I keep thinking about Hawthorne, dying in his sleep at near sixty. He lost his mind in his last year. He couldn't even recall the names of his characters. It saddens me, being the same age" (Caputo, 159). Both Styron and Hawthorne as writers share that sense of guilt which haunts the interior of Gothic romances, and so the connection is not all that farfetched or frivolous.

A few days before Styron entered the hospital, after he had given up drinking and after psychotherapy and antidepressant medications hadn't worked, he experienced, during a walk through the woods, Baudelaire's "wind of the wing of madness":

One bright day on a walk through the woods with my dog I heard a flock of Canada geese honking high above trees ablaze with foliage; ordinarily a sight and sound that would have exhilarated me, the flight of birds caused me to stop, riveted with fear, and I stood stranded there, helpless and shivering and aware for the first time that I had been stricken by no mere pangs of withdrawal but by some serious illness. I couldn't rid from my mind the line that for days had been skittering around at the edge of my consciousness: Baudelaire's "I have felt the wind of the wing of madness." (Frankiel, H17)

One remembers the birds in Peyton Loftis's monologue in *Lie Down in Darkness,* suggesting sexual guilt and the prelude to suicide.

In many ways such depression lies at the dark center of Styron's fiction. He himself has admitted, "I've come to think that mental illness and suicide has [*sic*] been a theme in my work. It must have been in my subconscious" (Frankiel, H17). One thinks of the Loftis family in *Lie Down in Darkness,* of Cass Kinsolving's rantings and "puddle of self" in *Set This House on Fire,* of Nat Turner's awareness of the loss of his faith and his abandonment by his God, of Stingo's darker perceptions and the labyrinthine web of guilt and suicide in *Sophie's Choice.* All of Styron's major characters have palpably suffered from feeling guilty for everything they have done. In a way, such depression has been the catalyst of Styron's fiction, and his characters have desperately had to face it, wrestle with it, at times triumph over and exorcise it. "Thus depression," Styron admitted, "when it finally came to me, was in fact no stranger, not even a visitor totally unannounced; it had been tapping at my door for decades."[5]

Events in Styron's life have certainly helped to accelerate if not cause the deep-seated melancholia of his own soul and that of his fiction. If heavy drinking and wrestling with the yet-unfinished novel *The Way of the Warrior* (which he may have been working on, on and off, since the fifties) contributed directly to his hospitalization in 1985, certainly his family background and his mother's death when he was just thirteen helped determine much of his attitude toward suffering and possible expiation. "The death of a parent," Styron explained, ". . . appears repeatedly in the literature on depression as a trauma sometimes likely to create nearly irreparable emotional havoc. The danger is especially apparent if the young person is affected by what has been termed 'incomplete mourning'—has, in effect, been unable to achieve the catharsis of grief, and so carries within himself through later years an insufferable burden of which rage and guilt, and not only dammed-up sorrow, are a part, and become the potential seeds of self-destruction" ("Darkness," 285).

"Both of my parents were depressives," Styron admitted to Caputo in 1985, "and people who have lost a parent early in life are more likely to get [the illness]. I lost my mother when I was a boy, so I had two strikes against me right there" (Caputo, 157). Pauline Margaret Abraham, from Uniontown, Pennsylvania, who had studied piano and voice in Vienna and taught music in public schools before her marriage to William Clark Styron, developed cancer shortly after her only child's birth and remained an invalid for the rest of her life. And Styron's father "battled the Gorgon for much of his lifetime, and had been hospitalized in my boyhood after a despondent spiraling downward that in retrospect I saw greatly resembled mine" ("Darkness," 285).

In "A Tidewater Morning," published in *Esquire* in August 1987, young teenager Paul Whitehurst—Whitehurst was Styron's paternal grandfather's middle name—must face up to the fact of his puritanical mother's agonized suffering, his father's cantankerous and alcoholic baiting of her, and her inevitable death. The parents fight over race, class, the father's southern background, and Paul's introverted existence before the mother finally dies. Throughout the story Paul can hear his mother's pain, the screams reverberating from her room upstairs, and he fully realizes, "My guilt was intensified by everything that was going on upstairs."[6] The father, "trying to mask the odor of alcohol," blurts out at the last: "In the incomprehensibility of my wife's agony I have found a terrible answer of sorts. If there is a God, he cares nothing for humankind" ("Tidewater," 95). Such a grim vision will dog the consciousness of most of Styron's main characters in his novels and may have served to feed the uprootedness and agonized self-analysis of *Lie Down in Darkness* and *Set This House on Fire*, before its ultimate culmination in *Sophie's Choice*.

Despite the battle with "the Gorgon," Styron revered his father, who died in 1978 and who appears in various guises in Styron's fiction as the voice of a lost rationality, a liberal southern gentleman at odds with the crass materialism of a consumer's world. William Clark Styron, for most of his life a cost engineer at the Newport News shipbuilding yards and an eloquent spokesman against the evils of monopoly capitalism, remarried soon after Pauline's death, and the stepmother, in Styron's eyes, seemed to be a desecration. It was Styron's adolescent disobedience and his drinking that may have resulted in his being sent in 1940 to boarding school, the Episcopal Christchurch, near Urbana, Virginia, on the Rappahannock River. He liked the familial and friendly atmosphere of the place but did not subsequently enjoy the repressive Presbyterian atmosphere of Davidson College. He did lose his virginity at the age of seventeen to a prostitute in a second-floor walk-up at the Green Hotel in Charlotte, North Carolina. Still, the cherished father figure in league with a new wife may have seemed an unforgivable betrayal to the young, "introspective" and bookish boy.

To the young Styron, his new stepmother, Elizabeth, "was as close to the wicked stepmother image as one can possibly imagine." From the family turbulence and his own anguish came the anguished intricacies of the self-indulgent lives of the Loftises in *Lie Down in Darkness:*

Lie Down in Darkness is a book which is really a mirror of the family life I myself put up with . . . the basic torment between Peyton and her family was really a projection of my own sense of alienation from my own tiny family—that is, my father, whom I really loved and this strange woman who had just come on the scene and who—I think I'm speaking as objectively as I can—was really trying to make my life a hell . . . at the age of 22 I remember being in a wildly unhappy state of neurotic *angst*. I had very few underpinnings. My emotional life was in upheaval. I'd lost what little faith I had in religion. I was just adrift, and the only thing that allowed me any kind of anchor was the idea of creating a work of literature [that] would also be a kind of freeing for me of these terrible conflicts that were in my soul.[7]

Styron has also acknowledged that it has been his wife, Rose, who has seen him through so much, that in fact she has been "the anchor . . . without her I would have been swept out to sea" (Frankiel, H17). In fact he has stated that during his clinical depression of 1985, "I became infantile—I didn't want her out of my sight."[8]

Styron's own southern background has obviously contributed to his outlook and fed his "terrible conflicts." His paternal grandfather, Alpheus Whitehurst Styron, was wounded in the Civil War on the Confederate side of the conflict, and he went on to become not only a pioneer steamboat operator but also a writer and reputable storyteller as well. Marianna Clark, Styron's paternal grandmother, grew up on a plantation in North Carolina and told her grandson of the two black girls who worked as her handmaidens. "All of us are bigots and racists at heart," Styron admitted in a televised interview with Dick Cavett in 1979. "We live in a racist era."[9] Add to that "an aspect of Southernness" that includes a sense of doom and guilt, the notion that the past is "very much a part of the present,"[10] and that "the WASP consciousness . . . generally speaking . . . has been tragic, at least serious in tone, adumbrated by Hawthorne's forest-gloom"[11]—and one should mention Faulkner's towering presence in this regard—and one can see the influence Styron's background certainly had on his vision of the modern world. It's almost as if his region and his self-consciousness reinforced each other, each supporting the darker aspects of the other.

Styron's generation, regardless of whether specific individuals actually participated in combat, experienced war and all its attendant anxieties both in World War II and in the traumatic circumstances of being recalled for the Korean War. For Styron, his wartime career seemed to conjure up his own mixed feelings about rebellion and authority, two distinct polarities of his consciousness that would haunt him throughout his fiction. In many ways these lie at the center of the "terrible conflicts that were in my soul." And the inadvertent blowing up by a stray mortar shell of eight young marine recruits at Camp Lejeune in 1951 and his own participation in a thirty-five mile forced march became ingredients for his second work of fiction, *The Long March*.

For years, perhaps since as early as 1953, Styron has struggled to fashion a long novel, tentatively entitled *Marriott, the Marine* and *The Way of the Warrior,* based on his wartime experiences and perceptions. Excerpts have appeared over the years, notably "Marriott, the Marine" in the September 1971 issue of *Esquire* and "Love Day" in the August 1985 issue of the same magazine. "A Tidewater Morning," published in the *Esquire* edition of August 1987, is described as "the introductory section for the novel he is now working on."[12] He has told interviewers, especially Philip Caputo, that after his hospitalization he updated the novel from its focus on World War II to one on the war in Vietnam. In June 1989 he stated, "I'm about halfway through it now" (Frankiel, H17). And as we know, his confinement, supposedly with syphilis, in the venereal disease ward at Camp Lejeune in 1944 was the focus of his only play, *In the Clap Shack,* which received mildly negative reviews.

As suggested, the experience in the Marine Corps seemed to emphasize Styron's own polarized attraction to and repulsion for both authority and rebellion, the Scylla and Charybdis of his fictional landscape. He once described himself as a "provisional rebel" (Coale), a provisionally tenuous statement in its own right: "I have been more or less drawn to human relationships in which there is a strong *polarity* of power and submission, or authority versus subservience. . . . I had a very strong streak of rebelliousness in me . . . later in the Marine Corps, I realized how powerfully I was repelled by authority myself. . . . I always had a very strong antiauthoritarian streak in me. It's a very profound resentment of authority. . . . It might be a *duality* because there's a part of me, at least at that time, that rather respected authority" [italics mine].[13] As one writer has suggested, "There is a proud, perhaps even haughty side to Styron—indeed, one suspects, the capacity to be obdurate."[14]

Polarities

One need not be versed in psychological labyrinths to be able to divine the oedipal tensions apparent in these polarized feelings and perspectives, another aspect of Styron's fiction. And such a sense of duality can easily play itself out in Styron's fictional methods and craft: "I think I've always been partially intent on contrasting the spiritual impulse as it is defined by Christianity with the hypocritical ritual and hypocritical shallowness and thought that surround much of its manifestations in life."[15] This view mirrors "the profound dualisms and ubiquitous paradoxes in America's major literature," as David S. Reynolds and others have firmly documented, "when moral systems are recognized as relative rather than unitary."[16]

In many ways Styron's literary career reflects the polarizations or dualities of his personality. For instance, *Set This House on Fire* was generally savaged by American critics—it was remaindered within a year of its publication in 1960—but the French enthusiastically embraced it. Maurice-Edgar Coindreau, Faulkner's first advocate in France, translated it as *La proie des flammes,* and it was published by Gallinard in February 1962. Styron soon became the only living author on the official list of English readings required for all French doctoral candidates, a list that also included Hawthorne, Poe, and Shakespeare.

The Confessions of Nat Turner was at first roundly applauded and celebrated, so much so that it went through six large printings in less than a year, the film rights were sold for $800,000, and it became Styron's first big commercial success. But then it was viciously denounced by black critics in *Ten Black Writers Respond,* an assault that Styron could never forget, one blasting Styron's conception of Nat Turner as a vacillating Uncle Tom, his supposedly inaccurate history, and his audacity for writing as a black slave. The denunciation became a cause célèbre in a racially charged and explosive era.

It was only the commercial and critical success of *Sophie's Choice* in 1979 that solidified Styron's literary reputation once and for all, despite some sniping from Jewish critics and others. Styron sold the film rights for $650,000, and Meryl Streep went on to triumph in Alan Pakula's film version. Yet even today Styron's reputation on college campuses, for instance, is shaky and uncertain, despite the extremely favorable responses of the vast majority of academics at the Seventh Winthrop Symposium on Major Modern Writers, "William Styron: Novelist and Public Figure." The symposium, held at Winthrop College in Rock Hill, South Carolina, in April 1986, eventually led to a special all-Styron issue of *Papers on Language and Literature* in 1987.

The man William Styron, though, still remains a very private individual, despite the public recognition of his battle with and apparent triumph over clinical depression. He himself has stated, "Time is the real healer and with or without treatment the sufferer usually gets well" ("Levi," A17). Yet the polarities in his personal makeup and the "provisional" rebelliousness of his earlier years suggest that there are still "terrible conflicts" within him, however carefully harnessed for fiction and for his own survival.

Polarities permeate Styron's life. He is the Southern Episcopalian who married the Jewish poet. He is the southerner who has lived most of his life in Connecticut. The "often violent nature of his writing [clashes with] his genteel country-squire style of life" (Caputo, 152). He is a white man who has written as a black, an only child who seems to crave connectedness and yet backs away from it, an antiwar marine, a man who at times seems sexually obsessed and who grew up in a sexually repressive era. Of his life at Davidson College, he once said, "My innate sinfulness was in constant conflict with the prevailing official piety."[17] He prides himself on paying obeisance to Flaubert's dictum: "Be regular and ordinary in your life, like a bourgeois, so that you may be violent and original in your work." In that regard it is interesting that William Styron presented John Cheever with the National Medal for Literature in 1982. Styron was once described as a man "abhoring intolerance but unwilling to fight actively against it or to work for any political cause."[18] He is a man in whom, it would seem, resistance breeds internal revolt and spiritual consciousness, believing that, as Czeslaw Milosz has put it in *The Captive Mind*, "even the enclosing fence affords the solace of reverie."[19] Authority and rebellion in Styron seem to require each other, so that he may dramatize and exorcise the ensuing collisions.

In discussing these polarizations in Norman Mailer's work, Joyce Carol Oates has suggested that such collisions can often produce paralysis, that such knotted, unresolved polarities can often produce constant repetitions and ceaseless oppositions. For Oates, Mailer's universe has become "a dualistic universe of irreconcilable forces. . . . [His] energetic Manichaeanism forbids a higher art. Initiation . . . brings the protagonist not to newer visions . . . but to a dead end, a full stop."[20] One wonders if such insightful criticism may apply in some cases to Styron and his work as well.

Styron's fiction obviously reflects such polarities. So many of his major characters spend their time musing about events that have already happened, trying to polarize the conflicts they see at the dark heart of things. *Sophie's Choice,* described by John Gardner, is "a piece of anguished Protestant soul-searching, an attempt to seize all the evil in the world—in his own heart first—crush it, and create a planet fit for God and man."[21] *Set This House on Fire,* for instance, has been described by critic Judith Ruderman as "a psychomachy, a war within the soul" (Ruderman, 120), and I think the description is apt.

Writes critic Norman Kelvin, "What Styron is best at creating is the pain of being a divided person. . . . It is a curious fact that Styron's novels elude the attempt to see them whole in the mind's eye. Nor do they create the impact of calculated discontinuity that would mark the intention behind them as modernist."[22] That dividedness is clearly rooted in American puritanical culture as well, as David Leverenz and others have made clear. The Puritans profoundly needed "to polarize ambivalence and to make authority secure. . . . Puritans responded to social mixture or conflict with a frame of oppositions." Like Styron, the Puritans habitually structured their vision of the world in terms of oppositions: "the ground for consent was clearly fixed in the Puritan mind: a fantasy of invisible male authority [God?] to which all on earth must conform or be cast out."[23]

And it is interesting to note that Freud's psychological view of existence is itself an extremely dualistic one, or as Douglas Robinson has described it, a basic "duel-ism": "Man's instincts, for Freud, are forever locked in conflict between life and death, a conflict that neither instinct can win until physical and mental death ends the instinctual struggle. . . . [Any] cure will be an illusion [and will be unable to transcend] the radical pessimism of Freud's antagonistic or dualistic concept of the psyche."[24]

For Styron, writing has always represented a form of therapy and self-analysis: "I'm emotionally fouled up most of the time. . . . When I'm writing I find it's the only time that I feel completely self-possessed—It's fine therapy for people who are perpetually scared of nameless threats as I am most of the time—for jittery people."[25] No wonder Marc L. Ratner suggested that "most of Styron's work . . . reflects his need to deal with his own neuroses."[26] Could Styron have been unconsciously trying to win back his father's love after his father remarried?

Throughout his career Styron has made much of the agony of writing. His deliberate and slow method may reflect the dark psychological weight of his themes, and he has admitted that he has had to "cast around for themes, there's no doubt about that" (Caputo, 150). "Writing is an awful profession, it really is . . . what you're doing is *confronting the unknown.* There's this blank paper. It's a corridor, it's a white corridor with no resonances, with no shadows, and down you go—Plunge!—for several years, trusting to your intuition . . . you might run into a dead end, and there's no way out."[27] He has also noted, "The process of writing has remained exceedingly painful,"[28] is "engendered by afternoons of vicious solitude,"[29] and is "sometimes almost hopeless" (Morris, 31). Whatever pleasure derived from it "is pretty much negated by the pain of getting started each day. Let's face it, writing is hell" (Matthiessen and Plimpton, 9). "I often have to play music for an hour in order to feel exalted enough to face the act of composing. I suppose it's a perfectionism."[30]

The long, slow process has never changed: "I average two-and-a-half or three pages a day, longhand on yellow sheets . . . about seven hundred, eight hundred words a day. . . . I seem to have some neurotic need to perfect each paragraph—each sentence, even—as I go along."[31] And yet, of course, "the art of writing is valuable, since, like music or sailing or drinking beer, it is a pleasure, and since at its best, it does something new to the heart" ("Prevalence," 47). Styron may be beguiling not only the reader by his voice.

Even Styron's awareness of literary generations carries oedipal tensions with it. Like so many of the post–World War II generation, he has admitted that, writing after the likes of Fitzgerald, Faulkner, and Hemingway, his generation took

longer to get out from under the shadow of its predecessors than probably any other literary generation. We were intimidated by the grandeur of these people, and I think we were unduly worried about our abilities to cope. . . . We are now grown men. *Don't* compare us with our predecessors. . . . I think I've realized I've achieved a voice. It may not be as striking as that of some of my predecessors, but who cares? . . . I don't think there's been any successor to Faulkner in terms of sheer protean genius and energy. . . . The point is that in our own way we are as good. ("Levi," 1988)

One can't help but notice the ambivalence writ large in such comments.

Perhaps the sprawl of *Set This House on Fire* best reveals Styron's state of mind at its most chaotic. "The man . . . is trying to glue himself back together," he once explained, "to put himself back together, to recollect himself if you wish . . . it's consciousness that's discontinuous."[32] The novel does reflect the "kind of chaotic wandering that I was enduring" (Coale). Styron acknowledged that he had "poured a lot of my life into it. . . . [It was] strangely put together . . . sagging, regrettable, immature lapses . . . [a kind of] crisis of identity. . . . I thought I was Harold Robbins or Irving Wallace. . . . [But] the effect on me of the criticism [was] hard to take."[33] And yet, said Styron, "For me, if literature cannot change the world in a radical way, it can, all the same, penetrate deeply into human consciousness."[34]

A sense of quest, founded and often foundering on the polarities in his personality and fiction, seems to continue to uphold Styron's life and art. He realizes that life becomes "increasingly difficult as we remove ourselves from old traditional environmental patterns," as he has done and as his characters have done as well in a fiction that mourns the loss of spiritual certainty and transcendent values (Coale). And yet he acknowledges, "Perhaps I'm grounded in some manner of unconscious transcendentalism that makes me believe people are striving for some impossible state" (Morris, 34). And he adds, "The quest after values, though dubious and vain, is preferable to paralysis,"[35] the object of which may not be as important as endurance itself.

That stoical notion of endurance and of an ongoing pursuit of values that continue to elude him seems to have sustained Styron—and continues to sustain him—in his own life. He has come out from under "a gray drizzle of unrelenting horror" and the "vague, spooky restlessness" that surfaced at their most extreme in his recent bout with clinical depression. The dark center of that depression seems always to have been with him. He has stared it down and written about it before. "Time is the real healer," he has written ("Levi," A17), and so evidently is his writing about it. A polarized soul, perhaps, can expect and do nothing less.

Chapter Two
Approaching Styron's Fiction

Over the years there have been several critical approaches to Styron's work as a whole. These have focused on his background as a southern writer, his use of the Gothic romance form, the acclaim of his work in France, his existential outlook on contemporary times, and his creation of guilt-ridden, anxiety-driven characters. Each of these approaches reveals an interesting facet of his fiction.

The Southern Imagination

William Styron has always been aware of his southern background and the traditions of writing in the South: "it . . . has to do with a sense of tradition, of ancestry, of family," he explained in 1968, "a sense of such matters as the importance of the Civil war to the history of the South, and the sense of literature as a continuous, continuing fountain . . . the idea of a respect for prose, a respect for literature as it is fed from the Bible—especially the old King James version—as a kind of cornerstone for the Southern ethos" (Barzelay and Sussman, 105). And because of that background he readily acknowledged that "any southerner is bound to suffer from a guilt complex."[1]

When *Lie Down in Darkness* was published in 1951, William Faulkner had just won the Nobel Prize (in 1950), and the existence and critical acceptance of the southern renaissance in American literature were already casting their long shadow. "I was very worried that [Faulkner] was going to affect my individuality as a writer," Styron admitted. "I had to leach him out of my system."[2] In *Sophie's Choice* Stingo also admits to "the influence of Faulkner"[3] in his first novel, *Inheritance of Night.*

Critics conjured up the roots and range of the southern context and imagination in order to come to grips with the phenomenon of the renaissance, and there was no way at that time that their judgment of Styron's first novel and of Styron himself could have escaped from that southern perspective. The southern imagination was a rural imagination thrust against the encroachment of the twentieth century. It sprang from exaggeration and biblical feats, spun in tall tales and laced with frontier humor. Its rhetorical sweep heightened reality in painting tragic and Gothic vistas of decay and moral destruction, what W. J. Cash in *The Mind of the South* referred to as romances "of the appalling." Defending the "peculiar institution" of slavery, many southern writers had justified it by recalling ancient societies and traditional ways.

As Frederick Hoffman suggests, southern tradition therefore remained "static . . . self-protective, and . . . encourage[d] fierce loyalties to its condition of being."[4] The southerners' preoccupation with history as they saw and celebrated it "would be a constant, the polestar of his journey . . . the plain farmer and fine planter would remain the men at the center of his message, the points around which the energies of his traditionalism seemed to gather."[5]

At the same time, because of its defensive position, its love of the concrete, and its sense of family and community, the South in its literature sought shelter in an emotional intensity that seemed to want to pass for knowledge and revelation of man's true place in the cosmic scheme of things. Such literature could also often degenerate into a kind of vague sentimentalism, a boundless nostalgia tied up with lost aristocratic graces, lush landscapes, and faded notions of gentility and propriety. As Allen Tate suggested, southern literature was often "about the people who are talking, even if they never refer to themselves, which they usually don't, since conversation is only an expression of manners, the purpose of which is to make everybody happy." From there to Tate's notion that "the rhetorical mode is related to the myth-making faculty, and the mythopoeic mind assumes that certain great typical actions embody human truth"[6] was not much of a logical leap. And the southern juggernaut of mythmaking, aligned with the South's sense of defeat and possible damnation, was complete.

Of course, there were cracks in the armor. James McBride Dabbs pointed out the fissure at the heart of southern society, the gap between (a) the aristocratic facade, with its paternalistic manners and plantation aspirations, and (b) the South's isolated, fundamentalist core, with its sense of human limitation, guilt, and sin, the stuff of many Methodist and Baptist circuit riders. What the South needed, according to Dabbs, was a hierarchical religion like Catholicism to buttress its aristocratic facade. What it produced, however, was an individualistic, grimly Protestant core, with racial slavery as the ultimate wedge between public image and private guilt. As Dabbs concluded, "The South never substantiated its soul. The South tried to live, on the one hand, by a highly social culture, on the other by a highly individualistic religion. The culture did not support the religion, the religion did not support the culture."[7] Within this southern mythical perspective, Styron published his first novel, and critics dealt with it accordingly.

In 1969 C. Vann Woodward took apart such "mythical" notions as Cash's "mind of the South" by attacking Cash's sense of unity and continuity in that mind and people. Woodward exploded the supposed homogeneity of southern sensibility by commenting on Cash's neglect of dissent in the South, on his failure to address antislavery sentiment, the two hundred thousand Southern Unionist dissenters who joined the Union Army, or the native black and white Republicans. To Woodward, southern history looked far more discontinuous than continuous. In effect Cash had succumbed to his own myth, "illustrating once more that ancient Southern trait which he summed up in one word, 'extravagent.' "[8] And yet Cash had also revealed the endurance and genuine importance of that myth of the solid South, however historically inaccurate it might have been. That myth was alive and well in much of Faulkner's fiction and in the developing criticism about the South in the 1950s; in that southern shadow appeared *Lie Down in Darkness* and the critical response to it.

Perhaps the apotheosis of Styron's own version of his southern background and the southern myth occurs in his thematic comparison between the South and Poland in *Sophie's Choice*. In Poland he finds "a beautiful, heart-wrenching, soul-split country" whose "indwellingly ravaged and melancholy heart" has been "tormented into its shape like that of the Old South out of adversity, penury and defeat." Both reveal "forlornly lovely, nostalgic landscape[s]" and "a poverty-ridden, agrarian, feudal society." Both have suffered defeat, which has bred in them "a frenzied nationalism." Both display "an entrenched religious hegemony, authoritarian and puritanical in spirit," as well as "the passion for horseflesh and military titles, domination over women (along with a sulky-sly lechery), a tradition of storytelling. . . . And being the butt of mean jokes" (*SC,* 247).

Pride and race have taken their collective toll. "Pride and the recollection of vanished glories . . . in ancestry and family name . . . in a largely factitious aristocracy, or nobility" haunt both regions, both of them overrun with carpetbaggers and other enemies. "In Poland and the South the abiding presence of race has created at the same instant cruelty and compassion, bigotry and understanding, enmity and fellowship, exploitation and sacrifice," as well as "centuries-long, all-encompassing nightmare spells of schizophrenia" (*SC,* 247–148).

Styron's fiction, then, has certainly been haunted by his southern imagination, bred as it seems to have been out of racial and racist relationships, religious rites of damnation and the search for a personal salvation, and a kind of incurable nostalgia and sense of loss embodied in the emotional swell and intensity of his melodious rhetoric, itself a product of the Bible Belt, tall tales of the southern frontier, and "a tradition of storytelling" from Augustus Longstreet and Mark Twain through Faulkner and Flannery O'Connor to Reynolds Price and Berry Fleming. Innumerable instances of race, religion, and rhetoric can be traced in Styron's fiction, and yet, as we shall see, his approach to his characters and material is far more contemporary and modern than that of writers we associate with the southern renaissance of the first half of the twentieth century.

The landscape and the rhetorical resonance of the southern imagination, as conjured up by Faulkner, are already completely visible and fully realized in *Lie Down in Darkness,* so much so that Styron's first novel seems at times no more than a variation on Faulknerian themes and tones, in Richard Gray's version "a cul-de-sac—a beautiful, spell-binding cul-de-sac admittedly, but a cul-de-sac nonetheless; and the gravity of its language, the brilliance of its structure—the impeccable nature, even, of its own self-reflexiveness—should never blind us to the fact that nearly everything in it is borrowed" (R. Gray, 290).

Here we find that "the ground is bloody and full of guilt where you were born"[9] and that the South's being "benighted . . . and the people filled with guilt" have produced "the very tragic essence of the land . . . rising from the ruins" (*LDD,,* 315–16). It is a Faulknerian place of decay and collapse, the kind of society that "should produce the dissolving family . . . with its cancerous religiosity, its exhausting need to put manners before morals. . . . Call it a *husk* of a culture" (*LDD,* 346). Milton Loftis's father can give the call to arms to be "a Southerner and a Virginian and of course a Democrat," with his antique notions that "especially Virginians" must wrestle with Christian ideals and "ideals inherent in you through a socio-economic culture over which you have no power to prevail" (*LDD,* 44), but it is a voice in the modern suburban wilderness of country clubs, golf courses, college football games, and "scene[s] of odious domesticity" (*LDD,* 51).

As in Faulkner's *The Sound and the Fury,* the blacks in *Lie Down in Darkness* act like a Greek chorus to the Loftis family, although Ella Swan's faith in Daddy Faith and her daughter, La Ruth, are often seen from a comic perspective, as are Daddy Faith's pretentious and rabble-rousing religious rites and baptisms, complete with trumpets and drums. Race rela-

tions are a given and take a backseat to the focus on the middle-class and
morose musings of the Loftis clan.

And Styron by no means entirely relinquishes his southern background.
The Long March takes place in the militaristic South. No matter how far
Cass Kinsolving and Peter Leverett travel in *Set This House on Fire,* they remain psychologically mired in an almost enervating nostalgia for their
southern roots, the landscape of their childhoods. All else seems a betrayal
of that celebrated and holistic sense of the past, so much so that Leverett's
father thinks the rest of the country needs "something to happen to it.
Something ferocious and tragic, like what happened to Jericho or the cities
of the plain,"[10] to awaken it from its materialistic and sexually exploitative
nightmare of the 1950s and return it supposedly to some quasi-religious
and necessarily "southern" truth. And in *The Confessions of Nat Turner,* of
course, Styron tackles his southern heritage in all its many manifestations,
both imprisoned by and exploding the southern myths that continued to
haunt him.

Race and racism have always played important roles in Styron's fiction,
from the essentially Greek-chorus perspective of the black maid at the end
of *The Long March* to the additional guilt Cass Kinsolving feels for burning
down a black cabin in *Set This House on Fire.* Even beyond *The Confessions
of Nat Turner,* Stingo manages to survive as a writer on the money he has
earlier received from the sale of a black slave, ironically named Artiste, and
Styron draws connections between Polish anti-Semitism and American
racism.

Styron's rhetoric is yet another reminder of his southern roots. "With
[Thomas] Wolfe alone I felt I had been captured by a demon," Styron
wrote, "made absolutely a prisoner by this irresistible torrent of language.
It was a revelation, for at eighteen I had no idea that words themselves—
this tumbling riot of dithyrambs and yawping apostrophes and bardic
cries—had the power to throw open the portals of perception, so that one
could actually begin to feel and taste and smell the very texture of
existence."[11] Often Styron produced such words for the sheer pleasure of
producing them, something like Dolly's love of Milton Loftis's talking in
Lie Down in Darkness, wherein "she found herself listening not so much
to the substance of what he said as to the tone of the words, the melodious, really endearing way he said it" (*LDD,* 66). Carey Carr may be a
bumbling unbeliever as a pastor, but "he was a sweet singer of the liturgy,"
and his "voice rose soft and sweet, insidiously compelling" (*LDD,* 257).
That voice will cause problems in *The Confessions of Nat Turner* and
Sophie's Choice, as it certainly did in *Set This House on Fire,* as Styron's

melodious rhetoric soars and swells and often seems delighted by its own resonance.

So Styron's southern roots are obvious, but the southern renaissance approach to his fiction doesn't really get us all that far. It leaves out the stranger, darker dilemmas of many of his characters, self-absorbed as they seem to be with their almost-undefined anxieties and guilts, their kind of "free-floating anxiety," that strike us as far more unnameable and disruptive than the anxieties that many of, say, Faulkner's characters experience. As Louis D. Rubin, Jr., suggested, Faulkner's Compsons' dooms "are dynastic, not personal. They are caused by history."[12] Faulkner's generational sense of a community's doom doesn't quite explain the more isolated and individual doom and often open rebellion we find in Styron's characters. As Jan B. Gordon describes it, Styron focuses more on that "part of a newer urban South where some ancient curse upon the land is replaced by some similarly ill-defined neurosis which afflicts the collective psyche."[13]

Perhaps the strongest argument in this regard has been made by Lewis P. Simpson. Styron's protagonists, he suggests, are "all versions of self-identity in extremis. . . . Styron dramatizes the anomalous self blindly seeking its apocalypse in the murder of what it cannot name."[14] Faulkner's narratives produce a communal effort within which characters are redeemed (or not) by linking past and present, by conjuring them up in communal situations rather than in isolated outposts of the individual spirit. Such characters become connected to a vast web of history and time, of memory and the past, and only then can they be fully understood or can we as readers begin to try to understand them. Styron's characters, on the other hand, realize only "the radical and mortal loneliness of each individual existence."[15] They grapple "with a gnostic modernity through the idea of the self as the constitutive realm of being"—a perceptive idea we will examine later in this chapter—and thus, in effect, Styron "dispossesses the South of Faulkner—that large and complex but special place of memory and history which Faulkner envisioned in his own way as an instruction to the soul, a bulwark against the dehumanization of man" (Simpson, 99–100).

In effect Styron's southernness, despite his southern sense of guilt and tragedy, intertwined as they are with race and religion, becomes the mere "husk of a culture" in his novels. The Faulknerian web of communal support and memory do not exist. The core of Styron's characters and his use of his material lie elsewhere, in a darker, more unexplored place where the critical notions of southern literature in general and the southern renaissance in particular fail to go. That renaissance provided a threshold to Styron's fiction, but if we seek to enter that fictional world more deeply, we must leave the southern myth and all it implies behind us.

The Gothic Romancer

In his review of *Sophie's Choice,* the novelist John Gardner wondered whether "the helpless groaning and self-flagellation of the Southern Gothic novel" (Gardner, 252) might not have been sufficient to deal with Auschwitz and the Nazi reign of terror, whether it was not, in Nathan Landau's perception of it, "a worn-out tradition" (*SC,* 115). In any case the critical exploration of the American romance as a separate genre, distinctly different from the more socially alert novels of the British, began in earnest with Hawthorne's definitions, in the prefaces to his books, between his romances and his novels; was picked up and expanded by such critics as Lionel Trilling, Richard Chase, and Michael Davitt Bell, beginning in 1950; and is still open to critical debate in the 1990s and beyond. That distinct generic tradition, coupled with a specifically southern Gothic vision, provides a more formal way of approaching Styron's fiction.

"The Southerner, as opposed to the Northerner, does not avoid but seeks melodrama," declared Leslie Fiedler, "a series of bloody events, sexual by implication at least. . . . The mode of the Southern is Gothic, American Gothic, and the Gothic requires a haunted house at its center. It demands also a symbolic darkness to cloak its action."[16] Irving Malin's discussions of Truman Capote, Carson McCullers, and Flannery O'Connor in his work on American Gothic fiction certainly indicate his agreement, and Francis Russell Hart's description of the Gothic almost coincides with the southern myth as described earlier, in its "fascination with time, with the dark persistence of the past . . . [a] hereditary curse . . . the cult of ruin . . . a world in ruins . . . the irrational, the primordial, the abnormal, and (tending to include the rest) the demonic" (quoted in Kerr, 4). Certainly Tony Tanner's description of American romanticism suggests the efforts many of Styron's own characters make in their own behalf, that "desire or compulsion to project the shape of one's own unique consciousness against the imprisoning shapes of the external world" (quoted in Kerr, 6).

Styron's novels share several of those characteristics of American Gothic romances which critics have pointed out since the tales of Edgar Allan Poe, Hawthorne's *The House of the Seven Gables,* and Melville's *Pierre,* through Faulkner's *Absalom, Absalom!* to name but a few. To begin with, we can locate, as Elizabeth M. Kerr suggests, "a Calvinistic Manichaean polarity of

good and evil and/or ambivalence in the moral attitude of characters"
(Kerr, 6) and in the almost-allegorical nature of Styron's characters, ar-
ranged as they are between what Marc L. Ratner has called the rebel-heroes,
like Peyton Loftis, Mannix, Cass Kinsolving, and perhaps Nathan Landau,
and the ineffectual, passive, but often sympathetic observers, like Milton
Loftis, Culver, Peter Leverett, and Stingo. Such a Manichaean vision paints
the world as a prison, an evil place not created by some good God but by
the devil, a place in which to confine man and from which he must try to
extricate himself. Over and over again Styron stalks the riddles of personality and sets up voices of "normalcy," moderate commentators, as clear-eyed
witnesses to extraordinary events and persons: Culver to Mannix, Leverett
to Kinsolving and Flagg, Stingo to Sophie and Nathan.

We find much the same dynamic in the often-Gothic relationships between Ishmael and Ahab in *Moby-Dick,* Nick Carraway and Jay Gatsby in
The Great Gatsby, and all the characters who tell in *Absalom, Absalom!* their
tales about Thomas Sutpen. The Gothic villain retains his central place in
the events that swirl around him as "a gloomy adult glowering out of his
isolation. . . . Necessarily, he is the aggressor, the oppressor of his innocent
victim."[17]

This ineradicable dualism in Styron's characters calls out for a kind of
Gothic allegorical treatment, perhaps revealing "a basic literary process reflecting fundamental tendencies of the human mind" (Robert Rogers,
quoted in Kerr, 7) in general and Styron's southern mind in particular.
Doubling is a technique and device long a product of the Gothic vision,
"born from the split and warring factions of the personality of the Gothic
villain" (MacAndrew, 50). And coupled with what Norman O. Brown has
called "the radical pessimism of Freud's agonistic or dualistic conception of
the psyche" (quoted in Robinson, 172), by which most writers of Styron's
generation have been influenced, we have a prescription for the psychologically Gothic romance that has remained so popular in twentieth-century
American literature, particularly in its southern guise.

"Gothic fiction is a literature of nightmare," explains Elizabeth
MacAndrew, a literature revealing "amorphous fears and impulses common
to all mankind . . . forbidding cliffs and glowering buildings, stormy seas
and the dizzying abyss" (MacAndrew, 3). One thinks of Sambuco in *Set
This House on Fire,* the pink palace in the Brooklyn of *Sophie's Choice,* and
perhaps in more muted tones the cell in which Nat Turner spends his final
days and the windowless, doorless white sepulcher of his dreams. "Dreams
are a very impressive part of my subconscious," Styron has said. "They linger
with me . . . and *seem* to be teaching me something" (Morris, 32). He elab-

orates in the same vein: "Fiction, which almost by definition is a kind of dream, often tells truths that are very difficult to bear, yet—again as in dreams—is able to liberate the mind through the catharsis of fantasy, enigma, and terror."[18]

Styron's recollections of Nat Turner's rebellion and his essay about his trip to Egypt suggest the kind of hypnagogic state that often begins one of Poe's tales. Styron has described himself as "haunted by that name [Nat Turner] I had first seen in the Virginia history textbook" (*TQD*, 14) and by blacks' impinging "upon [the southerners'] collective subconscious to such a degree that it may be rightly said that they become the focus of an incessant preoccupation, somewhat like a monstrous, recurring dream" (*TQD*, 10). At the conclusion of his essay on Nat Turner, "This Quiet Dust," he re-creates a moment of Gothic nightmare: "For an instant, in the silence, I thought I could hear a mad rustle of taffeta, and rushing feet, and a shrill girlish piping of terror; then that day and this day seemed to meet and melt together, becoming almost one, and for a long moment indistinguishable" (*TQD*, 30). It is the terror, the *frisson* of that Gothic moment that concludes the essay, as free from any moral value or metaphysical quest for truth as the best of Poe's similar moments.

Another such moment occurs on the Nile:

But I could go back to the Nile over and over, as if in mysterious return homeward, or in quest from some ancestral memory that has been only partially and tantalizingly revealed to me—as at that interval when one passes from sleep to waking . . . a quick flood of recognition, that I feel certain that *I have been here before,* in some other century. . . . And then I wonder how many others—hypnotized like me by this river and the burden of its history, and by the drama of the death along its shores and waters, and eternal rebirth in all—might have known the same epiphany. (*TQD*, 171)

The hypnagogic state, the Poesque *frisson,* the center of a dark dream full of revelation, self-hypnosis, the burden and drama of history and death, the river itself: what is this but essentially the dark dreamscape of Gothic romance? One thinks of Helen Loftis's dream of corpses in *Lie Down in Darkness,* of Nat Turner's dream of the unbroken white facade of the temple on the hill, of Cass Kinsolving's dreams of dissolution and evil intruders in *Set This House on Fire,* of Sophie's nightmares of guilt and doom.

Other devices of the Gothic romance appear in Styron's fiction. The rhetoric, embodying visions of doom and destruction, full of fateful omens and auguries, we've already touched upon. But Styron also relies often on the first-person narrator, the visible narrator who undergoes a transformation in character and perceptions because of entering into the nightmarish realm of other, demon-haunted characters, such as Peter Leverett, Stingo, and even, to some extent, Nat Turner in his meditation on his lost cause and solitary murder. And such transformations often take place in remote, mysterious settings, those closed worlds such as Sambuco and the Brooklyn pink palace which suggest "the isolated world of the self" (MacAndrew, 119).

Styron's narrative structure also parallels that of the Gothic romance, as it moves from revelation to revelation, surprise to surprise, climax to climax, each more shattering than the preceding one. "All this puts us on notice that a mysterious world is about to be revealed," suggests Elizabeth MacAndrew, ". . . a cumulative system of narration that creates the impression of a gradual but steady piecing together of the truth" (MacAndrew, 11, 128). MacAndrew concludes in her discussion of Mary Shelley's *Frankenstein* that "the concentric, nested system of narration leads from the everyday world . . . until buried in the center we come to the strangest of them all, that of the monster's account" (MacAndrew, 145).

At the end of Styron's often labyrinthine narrative corridors and "nests," we come to the monstrous revelations of Peyton's suicide, Cass's murder of Mason Flagg, Nat's murder of Margaret Whitehead, and Sophie's surrender of her daughter Eva to the gas ovens of Birkenau. We have almost reached that place at the end of Poe's "The Fall of the House of Usher," wherein, according to Lewis Simpson, "Southern writing tends to record the breakdown of the endeavor in reconstruction" and leaves us with that dark "covenant with the self as the sole source of memory and the total meaning of history" (Simpson, 71, 68).

The lingering problem with Styron's Gothic climaxes, however, has to do with how we are to interpret them. Both Robert Dale Parker and Gordon Hutner discuss, respectively, Faulkner's and Hawthorne's skillful repression of secrets within their narratives as a way of involving the reader in the unmasking of veils, in the search for and interpretations of a complex truth about the nature of the human heart in conflict with itself. Such narrative repressions also increase the necessity of revelation, and they force the reader to sympathize with the characters involved. In some cases, according to Hutner, Hawthorne deliberately keeps the secrets about his characters' pasts as vague and insubstantial as possible, so that the reader comes to understand the full ambiguity of human experience and to recognize that "the play of ambiguity is seemingly endless." Such ambiguities "signal the reader's response, as Hawthorne wants to shape it, to a world of intrinsic mystery."[19]

But for the most part, with the revelations made and the demonic or demon-haunted characters murdered (Mason Flagg, Nat Turner) or having committed suicide (Peyton Loftis, Sophie and Nathan), Styron ends his Gothic exorcisms in an upbeat, optimistic manner. This aspect raises the question of whether or not that optimism has been earned, whether or not "like melodrama [instead of genuine tragedy], with which it has much in common, the popular Gothic romance arouses sham terror and has a reassuring happy ending" (Kerr, 3).

The endings of *Set This House on Fire*, *The Confessions of Nat Turner*, and *Sophie's Choice* reveal some remarkably similar imagery, as if Styron were trying to escape the nightmares he had conjured up. At the end of *Set This House on Fire*, his most Manichaean romance, Cass spies at dawn the fishing boats on the gulf and sees "these lights moving across the water like a crowd of stars adrift" (*SHF,* 508). Nat Turner awakens at dawn and "stand[s] motionless in the still-encompassing dark. . . . I raise my eyes upward. There . . . shines the morning star . . . steadfast the morning star rides in the heavens." And he concludes, "Oh how bright and fair the morning star."[20] And Stingo at the end of *Sophie's Choice* awakens to stare at a "tiny orb of crystal, solitary and serene, Venus. . . . It was then that in my mind I inscribed the words: '*Neath cold sand I dreamed of death/but woke at dawn to see/in glory, the bright, the morning star*" (*SC,* 515). In each of these books the coming of the star signals the conclusion of the nightmare, however gentle the ironies that surround its coming.

The problem with pegging Styron as "merely" another Gothic romancer is that, again, doing so leaves out too much. Gothic fiction isolates the self in all its turbulent fears and demonic dreams. It suggests that society and history are merely psychological projections of some primordial, nightmarish self that can recognize only its own claustrophobic world. Styron is clearly attempting to grapple with larger historical issues, such as racial slavery and the Holocaust; with "the individual's revolt and outrage against the system"; and with the "violation of the individual by the demands of [such] institutions"[21] as the military, the contemporary consumer society, anti-Semitism, and racism. He is clearly wrestling with, in his own words, "a form of human domination that seems to be a constant in human history."[22] That constant includes "the catastrophic propensity on the part of human beings to attempt to dominate one another" (Eubanks, 274). And he seems riveted by his vision "that even in the midst of an ultimate process of dehumanization the human spirit cannot be utterly denied or downed" (*TQD,* 301).

Whether or not Styron succeeds in accomplishing this vision of domination and deliverance is, at the moment, another story. But such reaching for a wider historical perspective cannot be thoroughly explained and explored by the reliance on formal Gothic devices or on descriptions of American romances as a specifically identifiable genre. Like the southern myth, descriptions of the Gothic romance can lead us further into the darker depths of Styron's fiction, but they don't exactly describe what's going on there. This formal and generic approach must finally fall short as well, since it must leave out many of the humanistic and historical dimensions of Styron's vision that elude the Gothic straitjacket.

The French Connection

Much has been made in recent years of Styron's literary reputation in France. The negative reviews in the United States of *Set This House on Fire*—so negative, perhaps, for Styron that the middle-aged Stingo in *Sophie's Choice* fails to mention this novel as one of the ones he has written or published—were more than transcended in France by the extremely positive response to *La proie des flammes* in 1962. And Styron's reputation in France since then has only continued to grow. From this wider perspective, we might be able to see a different Styron, beyond one bounded merely by American terms like "the Myth of the South" or by the American version of Gothic romance.

In his *A French View of Modern American Fiction* Maurice Edgar Coindreau, the translator of Faulkner into French, describes clearly what the French saw in Faulkner, an indication of the literary context in which they read Styron's later novels. In his preface to *Sanctuaire,* Faulkner's first novel published in France, in 1934, Andre Malraux wrote, "Faulkner buries himself in the irremediable . . . perhaps the irremediable is his only true subject."[23] Something irremediable is something incurable, incapable of being relieved, of correcting or counteracting evil, of obtaining redress for a wrong. One thinks easily of the atmosphere of *Lie Down in Darkness* and *Set This House on Fire.* Coindreau praises Malraux for discovering depths in *Sanctuary* that American critics had missed.

The sense of psychological and epistemological depth, of the tragic view of life, and of a fatality enveloping the world, discovered in Faulkner's fiction by the French, becomes for modern French criticism the touchstone for later American writers. "Faulkner exteriorizes the things that swarm in the lower regions of the human soul," Coindreau writes, and—in his 1954 preface to William Goyen's *The House of Breath* (*La maison d'haleine*)— defines the younger American writers as "born disillusioned or rather gifted

with tragic insight," explaining that "one must go courageously all the way
to the depths . . . seize the beast, and dominate it by forcing it out into the
full light of day" (Coindreau, 69, 132–33).

Such newer American writers, Coindreau notes, "all bow before William
Faulkner, whose descents into hell are at once an inspiration and a danger to
them," and must "travel the road that Hawthorne had indicated . . . the
study of [in Faulkner's words] 'the human heart in conflict with itself.' " To
prove his point Coindreau mentions, after praising such writers as Carson
McCullers and Truman Capote, the fact that he'd asked Styron why Styron
had remained silent for so long between *Lie Down in Darkness* and *Set This
House on Fire*. Styron replied, "I wanted to free myself from Faulkner's influence before starting another full-scale book. *The Long March* was my disintoxication exercise" (Coindreau, 134, 104).

French critics also praised Faulkner's poetic style, viewing it in terms
often reserved to discuss the symbolist poets, such as Baudelaire and
Mallarme. Coindreau describes that style as "loaded and sometimes over-
loaded with images, interrupted by interminable incidents which follow the
slow progress of thought, the meanderings of introspection and the sinuosi-
ties of analysis" (Coindreau, 70). Again it is relatively easy to recall Cass
Kinsolving's long and often-tedious monologues in such a context.

Thus the French argument in favor of Faulkner's fiction clears the path
for the ones in praise of Styron's. The depth, often diabolic in its lack of re-
prieve, of the human heart in conflict with itself; the dark designs of a guilt-
ridden, obsessive puritanism; the often convoluted and rhetorical diction of
poetry—Faulkner, once thought of as "only an emissary of the devil"
(Coindreau, 11)—in France becomes Styron's emissary as well.

But there is an older emissary than Faulkner who furnished a literature
for the French to praise and describe as eminently the best of American literature. Faulkner, writes Coindreau, "continues the line of such writers as
Edgar Allan Poe," just as Truman Capote can be viewed as "a brother of the
great anxiety-ridden men of literature: Baudelaire, Mallarme, and especially
Edgar Allan Poe" (Coindreau, 32, 129). In effect the French's appreciation
of Poe paved the way for their appreciation of Faulkner and set the stage for
the French vision of the best that American literature has to offer.

Poe conjured up his diabolic designs in an hallucinatory and poetic style,
the kind the symbolist poets celebrated, a style formulated by Baudelaire in
his fascination with the American writer. Poe's use of certain words for certain effects in many ways parallels Styron's own. Both appreciate the relation between language and music and would agree that passionate language
itself becomes musical.

In *Set This House on Fire* Mason Flagg embodies many American evils in Styron's creation of him: the lust for material wealth; the lust for endless lust itself; the need to dominate others, to humiliate and feed off them in some vampiric manner; the rage for the consumer society of the 1950s to glory in its objects and its goods. And in France Styron has often been seen as an exile in his own land, a prophet in the wilderness that is his own country.

The author as literary martyr, as exile in a land blighted by American materialism, is an image that has perfectly suited the likes of Poe and Faulkner both at home and in France. Baudelaire was drawn to this very aspect of Poe and viewed him as an outlaw, as "a long-suffering soul of great nobility, asphyxiated by an ignoble culture."[24] In his first preface to Poe's tales, Baudelaire wrote in a letter to Sainte-Beuve in 1856: "I tried to include a sharp protest against Americanism. . . . [Poe] reveals almost anti-American thinking. Moreover, he mocked his compatriots to the best of his ability."[25]

Coindreau picked up the same myth in the 1950s and early 1960s. Americans were either millionaires or redskins before the introduction of Faulkner and modern American literature. Americans want only "to learn how to enjoy the present"; they seem to see themselves as "virtuous by definition"; and they inhabit "a country where exhibitionism and social promiscuity are raised to the dignity of civic virtues" (Coindreau, 106, 104, 109).

Unfortunately, Styron's French reputation, admirable though it is, doesn't get us much further into the works themselves. It seems to be too similar to ideas and images contained in the explications of the southern renaissance and the American Gothic romance. The French seem to have an affinity for both in their celebration of Poe and Faulkner and Styron, a line of literary descendants that seems predicated on the notions of Gothic depths, poetical style, tragic muses, and obsessive puritanical designs. None of this approach is necessarily wrongheaded, but it does seem to "re-heat" the same arguments we've discussed earlier in this chapter.[26]

Perhaps the only French perspective that can put a new slant on Styron's fiction is the philosophical one of existentialism. And for this it might be best to look at both Sartre's and Camus's versions of it.

The Existentialist

Briefly summarized, for Sartre existence precedes essence; therefore there are no a priori values, and ultimately God may not exist. Sartre's definition of existence rests heavily on Descartes's notion of subjectivity, "I think;

therefore I am." That subjectivity encompasses all of man's freedom of choice, the necessity to invent and create himself in action. At the same time, such actions reveal the existence of other selves, other men and women, and thus connect the individual to his fellow man. Since man is the only "being which *is* in such a way that in its being its being is in question" and is the only "being which is compelled to decide the meaning of being,"[27] with man's subjective existence come both ultimate freedom and responsibility.

This existent self faces a meaningless universe, an absurd world within which the self and that world are locked in endless contradictions and unrelieved tensions and anxieties. There will always be a gap between the self's intention and its execution of that intention, a continuing frustration and forlornness. But Sartre surmounts the potential grimness of the confrontational situation by declaring, "Live the conflict, for only the conflict can make you free."[28]

All man's choices and decisions necessarily involve anguish and an unrelieved sense of one's own isolation and alienation in the scheme of things. Yet the self locates within itself a transcendency, a desire to pass beyond, to strive toward some wider goal that, despite ultimate frustration and the limitations of death and mortality, represents what Sartre describes as "the desire to be God" (Sartre, 69). This desire, Sartre concludes, represents not a universal human nature but the universal human condition.

David Galloway, in applying existential notions to his first study of Updike, Bellow, Salinger, and Styron in *The Absurd Hero in American Fiction* (1966), understandably focuses on Camus's *The Myth of Sisyphus* and emphasizes the heroic potential in the existential conflict of the rebel-hero: "Like Camus, these authors reject nihilism and orthodoxy, and like Camus too, they end by affirming the humanity of man. The absurd hero is by definition a rebel" (Galloway, 15).

Within such broad existentialist perspectives, Styron's characters at first do seem to fit. Nat Turner, abandoned by his God in his jail cell, certainly feels isolated and alienated and believes that all values have been taken from him. He confronts a new void in his existence, as well as the uncertain connections between his religious values and the failed insurrection he has led. Likewise Cass Kinsolving, dissolving in his "puddle of self," feels "sick unto death" (*SHF*, 276) and faces a universe in Sambuco of unrelieved suffering and irremedable grief, so much so that it borders on the absurd and the unknowable. Mannix, too, perceives the absurdity of his rebellion in *The Long March,* and Sophie, nearly paralyzed by her sense of guilt and doom, must confront the shocking consequences of her choices, including all the anguish and horror those choices have left her with.

In his chapter, "The Absurd Man as Tragic Hero," Galloway views Styron's characters as tragic heroes, employing the notion that the optimistic essence of tragedy affirms a moral order superior to the individual, but the title of Richard Lehan's essay may be closer to American interpretations of existentialism: "Existentialism: The Demonic Quest." Lehan suggests, "Destruction—either death or a kind of insanity—is at the end of the existential quest. And yet the quest . . . is absolutely necessary." What the hero desires is "to be so self-involved that the outside world is no longer a threat" (Galloway, 78), such a solipsistic position that it seems to create an even greater sense of alienation and isolation than the conditions that preceded such a state. And yet Lehan in his discussion of Sarte, Camus, Bellow, Wright, and Ellison does define existentialism broadly enough to include many of Styron's characters: "All are concerned with the meaning of identity in the modern world, the nature of good and evil, the possibility of fulfillment in the contemporary society, the source of values in a world without God, and the possibility and meaning of action in an ethical vacuum" (Galloway, 64).

Styron's own comments involve Camus more than Sartre and may be far more revealing. In a 1963 letter to Pierre Brodin, Styron wrote, "Of the moderns of any nationality, including the United States, Camus has had the largest effect upon my thinking, and I have valued the quality of his *moral intensity* more than anything I have found in any other contemporary. Consequently, I believe certain French attitudes have entered my writing [italics mine]" (quoted in Ratner, 136). He also acknowledged Camus's direct influence on *The Confessions of Nat Turner:*

I had just read for the first time Camus's "The Stranger." It is a brilliant book, the best of Camus, and it impressed me enormously: there was something about the poignancy of the condemned man sitting in his jail cell on the day of his execution—the existential predicament of the man—that hit me. And so did the use of the first person. . . . The effect of all this was so strong that I suddenly realized that my Nat Turner could be done the same way: that, like Camus, I would center the novel around a man facing his own death in a jail cell (Galloway, 107).

Noticeably it is the "moral intensity" that intrigues Styron, the "poignancy" of the condemned man in the jail cell, a kind of existential situation that may have little to do with either Sartre's more philosophical notions or existentialism in general.

But the question still remains: is Styron an existentialist? Does his fiction operate in a world best described as existentialist? And are his characters motivated by existentialist concerns and grievances? It seems to me that the answer to these questions is probably no, since there is still too much of Styron's vision that lies outside existential domains.

For one thing, none of Styron's characters show or cultivate the kind of "lucid indifference" that Camus's characters and Sartre often do. Certainly Styron's prose does not do so in the way that Hemingway's but especially Camus's prose does seem to do. If, as one critic has suggested, "L'homme absurde is a man without nostalgia" (Galloway, 13), then Styron's characters and his nostalgia-celebrating prose do not partake of existential absurdity. Perhaps indifference is a far more European trait, especially in postwar Europe, than it is an American one.

Styron is too caught up in offering explanations within his fictions for his characters's dilemmas, explanations that offer specific values and concepts, however muddled they may be when taken as a whole. Whether Styron or just his characters see themselves from the perspective of Christian humanism, in which personal redemption and damnation do matter, is something to be examined in more detail later in this chapter, but certainly his fiction is filled with Christian descriptions, images, and tag lines. Stingo's "voyage of discovery" does end in a kind of expiation; he undergoes a personal exorcism and commits neither murder nor suicide. An aura of tragedy does hover around his growing awareness of the world at large. And Styron, like many novelists of his generation, all too often relies on Freud to see him through, as if Eros were battling Thanatos in a predetermined Freudian "duel-ism," with the outcome already decreed. In many instances, as we'll see, the psychological explanations often threaten to undermine the more tragic-religious aspects in his fiction.

Styron, however dark his vision of the world, seems to retain a basic American optimism. After all, Nat Turner does experience a revelation of sorts just before his execution, however ironic that revelation may appear to the reader. And both Cass Kinsolving, who did, after all, murder Mason Flagg, and Stingo manage to come through their ordeals, chastened but intact. Because American culture may be an "essentialist" culture, based as it is on certain myths of progress and possible redemption, is that why it seems so difficult for Styron to shake off such myths? Because the culture is so much nourished, for good or ill, by such myths and less by the connections between tribal bloods and ethnic certainties, is that the reason Styron can still keep his eye on the morning star after the nightmare has ceased?

At the core of Styron's fiction lurks a pervasive guilt that neither Sartre nor Camus really discusses or touches upon. That guilt corrodes all it invades or inhabits, as if it were a kind of ontological human condition that will always exceed any causes Styron can try to locate in his characters's lives or their society. It is, as Cushing Strout describes it, "the pressure Americans felt—and still feel—to exaggerate their guilt, while minimizing their political responsibility, through a vision of history which wavers between a nightmare of doom and a dream of utopia."[29] Such pressure stems from viewing life as an essential drama involving personal redemption and damnation, a Puritan hangover of lasting consequence.

Notions of guilt, expiation, and exorcism may get us closer to the heart of Styron's vision. These seem to transcend the limitations placed on them by the southern myth, the Gothic romance, much of French criticism, and Sartre's existentialism. Styron's characters do not suffer from some Faulknerian sense of communal loss and bifurcated cultural memory; they are not merely obsessed characters in the Gothic mode; nor are they existentialist souls living the conflict simply to make themselves free. There is more here, more to Styron's vision of the self, and perhaps in our discussion of that element we can get even closer to the heart of darkness and source of torment in his fiction.

The Encapsulated Self

At the center of Styron's fictional realm there exists a self or sense of a fictional character that none of the aforementioned critical theories has yet been able to define. This self swells beyond the boundaries placed on it by its innate southerness, its Gothic obsessiveness, and its existential isolation. Styron's characters tend to overwhelm the fictional universe they inhabit. They swallow it up in their sense of anxiety, guilt, doom, self-scrutiny, and self-evisceration, a process that often verges on the narcissistic and solipsistic. In an attempt to trace the origins of this self, perhaps we can draw closer to the kind of strange creature it appears to be.

The seeds for this self may have been sown in the postwar world of the late forties and fifties in the United States. The cold war era had dawned and was becoming firmly entrenched in the popular mind. Donald Pease, for instance, in his *Visionary Compacts* (1987) tries to assess all major American literary criticism of the period as a response to the "global scenario popularly designated as the Cold War,"[30] when it attempted to view the major literature of the American renaissance as a battle between individual freedoms and totalitarian wills, thus losing sight of the genuine desire of those renaissance writers to restore a sense of community in the pre–Civil War querulousness of the 1850s. Russell Reising believes that after World War II was over, "the theme of absolute good versus absolute evil was retained by simply putting the Bolshevik in place of the Hun as the menace to democracy everywhere, a simplistic and falsely moralistic interpretation."[31] Ronald Reagan's "Evil Empire" spoke to this particular morality play.

As a result of viewing the world divided into two warring camps, many writers and intellectuals regarded the individual self as a far more complex and ambiguous entity than that scenario would allow. The 1950s spawned a kind of muted religious revival, a return to the neo-orthodox ideas of innate depravity, of human sin and human limitation, a darker image of the self that underscored both American and Soviet camps. In effect the neo-orthodoxy of the fifties upended what seemed to be the social materialism of the twenties and thirties—particularly in literary criticism—and "transferred the grounds of reality from economic and political *systems* to human *psyches*" (Reising, 95). The self or soul became the true place where realities began; the rest became mere social facade and political propaganda.

In writing about Styron and the "Fiction of the Fifties," David L. Stevenson in 1960 described Styron as writing "the peculiarly bleak, uncomforting, largely a-social novel of the fifties." He quotes a *Time* reviewer's assessment in 1951 of *Lie Down in Darkness* as "one more recruit for the dread-despair-and-decay camp of U.S. letters." Setting aside the usual existential trappings of Stevenson's essay, what does come clear from his point of view is Styron's evocation of "a world of complex, half-conscious perceptions, feelings, attitudes concerning the meaning of love and sex" and his wrestling with "ultimate questions" in the face "of the Stygian chaos and old night" and the unconditional in man. Such a vision proves that "our new generation of literary artists have abandoned social man for the unconditioned in man."[32]

After the political disruptions of the 1960s, that self seems to have reasserted itself in the doctrines of "enlightened" selfishness and the boisterous anxieties of the "me decade," culminating in the eight-year reign of Ronald Reagan. People have become so inner directed by now, the criticism goes, that that's all there is; the social scene has essentially vanished and been swallowed up at an omnivorous, narcissistic feast.

The criticism has mounted in the recent past with Christopher Lasch's damning of American culture as a "culture of narcissism" (1979), portraying only "the subjective experience of emptiness and isolation."[33] Robert Bellah and his colleagues in the popular sociological tract *Habits of the Heart* (1985) belabored Americans' fascination with self-interest only, leaving "the individual suspended in glorious, but terrifying isolation,"[34] victimized by managerial techniques and temporarily assuaged by therapists' latest programs. And Alan Bloom in his gloomy assessment of *The Closing of the American Mind* (1987), blaming Nietzsche and Heidegger as popularly influential atheists, describes Americans as mesmerized by "the self, the mysterious, free, unlimited center of our being. All our beliefs issue from it and have no other validation. . . . The ego is all there is."[35]

The surfeited self of the eighties at first looks far different from the neo-orthodox, sin-ridden self of the fifties, but in effect the fascination with self-scrutiny remains remarkably similar, however less apocalyptic than critics would suggest. Styron's early guilt-ridden characters certainly seem to be spawned from neo-orthodoxy and original sin, even though their emotional sense of their guilt and despair overrides any definable moral or religious scruples and exists in a more free-floating, breast-beating manner. Still, the self has always been an American obsession, conceived as it was as something to be created and shaped by a new culture in a new environment. One need only look back at de Tocqueville's analysis of the new democratic self in the 1830s to see that the vision of the individualistic and self-oriented self was always an American concern.

In effect Styron's focusing on the individual self puts him squarely in an American literary tradition. This focus is not in itself unusual or strange; however, in many ways that self may be all there is in Styron's fiction, despite the laboring to connect it to such great and horrible historical events and institutions as racial slavery and the Holocaust.

What surfaces again and again in reading the fiction is the vision of the encapsulated self, a self so self-enclosed that no matter how it tries to connect with others, it is so mired in its own problems or visions that it nearly drowns in them. Nat Turner, for instance, is brutally encapsulated by the institution of racial slavery in Virginia, yet he spends so much time wrestling with his personal relationship to God and sex that this activity seems to blind him to the very institution that victimizes him. Likewise Stingo in *Sophie's Choice* spends so much time grappling with his sexuality and his desire to be a writer that Sophie's horrifying victimization at the hands of the Nazis seems almost to exist only as an effort to break through Stingo's own self-concerns to let him know that the world is not only evil but a power to reckon with beyond his own self-scrutinies. Cass Kinsolving's "puddle of self" capsizes *Set This House on Fire,* despite his murder of the willfully narcissistic Mason Flagg. And the Loftises are so at sea in self-recriminations and guilt that they seem trapped like flies in amber in a self-indulgent world gagging on its own undefinable, selfish fixations.

Guilt, Styron's awareness perhaps of neo-orthodox notions of sin, exists as the irremediable anguish and remorse of self-reproach resulting from the sense that one has done something wrong for some real or imagined offense or crime. And no amount of expiation or exorcism, unless hedged by morning stars and existential tag lines, seems able to overcome it.

Guilt, however vague, unanchored, and all-pervasive, lies at the core of the self in Styron's fiction. Trying to track it down to its source—and not leaving it free-floating, as if it were an existential truth we should just take for granted—may help us understand what's going on here. And it is the scope of guilt, finally, and not the recognition of guilt itself, that may be the source of uncertainty and consternation.

"The new psychiatric wisdom . . . has contributed . . . toward the introspective in fiction," Styron explained early in his career (quoted in Ratner, 56). And Marc Ratner may have described the situation exactly when he wrote, "Most of Styron's work has its basic psychological roots in the Oedipal situation and . . . it reflects his need to deal with his own neuroses." Such a situation may reveal "the failure of the father and, by implication, the children's avoidance of responsibility" (Ratner, 56, 54). "Perhaps," as Styron himself has said, "the miseries of our century will be recalled only as the work of a race of strange and troublous children, by the wise old men in the aeons which come after us" (M. West, 218–19). Thus, as Ratner's argument continues, "Styron . . . presents heroes who struggle to liberate themselves from childishness and from a system which keeps them children" (Ratner, 56).

The evidence is everywhere apparent. Milton and Helen Loftis compare themselves with and often despise their fathers. Peyton feels her father is smothering her, and her only out is suicide. Mason Flagg's relationship with his mother, Wendy, is downright incestuous, and Peter Leverett treats his father's embittered pronouncements all too seriously. Nat Turner must wrestle with all kinds of fathers, from Sam Turner to God, each seemingly benign and suddenly gratuitously cruel but always omnipotent. And in *Sophie's Choice* Stingo wrestles with his southern father's wisdom, while Sophie joins her professor-father in his blatant and virulent anti-Semitism.

John Kenny Crane in his discussion of "Styron's Father Figures" sees each one of them as "moral and God-fearing, each is attuned to the decay of the modern world and the ambiguous glory of the past . . . out of synch with the times,"[36] excluding Sophie's father. And Richard Gray in his discussion of Styron's southern legacy in his fiction describes *Lie Down in Darkness* as "an elegy, or imitative tribute, to the father figure [Faulkner] of modern Southern literature" (R. Gray, 289). At the same time, Styron has consistently confirmed as much and remarked on his conscious attempts to wean himself from that incestuous rhetorical embrace.

In 1969 Styron described himself as a "provisional rebel" (Coale), and the phrase has continued to haunt my image of him. In rebelling against the system, many of Styron's characters go on to rebel against their own rebellions, as if, like children, they can rebel only on another's terms or only within the boundaries of another's authority. Mannix mimics Templeton in his rebellious persistence in *The Long March*. Peyton Loftis's rebellion is just as wayward and self-indulgent, just as moody and uncertain, as her father's. Cass can exorcise his demons and get off the hook at the same time. Nat Turner questions the nature of his rebellion all along and cannot act when the time comes, more aware of the psychological-religious traumas of his visionary self than the rightness of his cause. And the real would-be rebels from whatever perspective die—Peyton Loftis, Mason Flagg, Nat Turner, and perhaps Sophie and Nathan.

Styron himself has said, "I have been more or less drawn to human relationships in which there is strong polarity of power and submission, or authority versus subservience" (Morris, 36). Perhaps that ambivalence is one of the sources of the guilt-ridden Styron persona, drawn both to rebellion and to devotion and torn emotionally between the two, with no clear-cut response to either. Social injustice does not really unbalance the querulous equilibrium, nor does a disinterest in social justice. Rather, the typical Styron character looks in both directions at once, muddled, anxious, telegraphing his own anguish with a vengeance.

Is it ambivalence that powers Styron's fictional world and the characters in it, and that in doing so creates a realm of guilt, anxiety, and unrelenting self-reproach? On the one hand, Styron exposes all the contradictions, paradoxes, and ambiguous drives in his larger-than-life characters and in doing so threatens to overwhelm the fictional world in which they function, reducing that world to omnivorous monologue, as in *Set This House on Fire,* or to first-person confessional, as in *Nat Turner* and *Sophie's Choice.* On the other hand, Cass and Stingo see themselves through; an exorcism or expiation of a sort is supposed to have taken place. But in order for this to happen, the not-so-secret "abomination" has to be suppressed, destroyed, just as Mason Flagg must be killed, and Sophie and Nathan must kill themselves. And in Nat Turner's strangely ambiguous deliverance at the end of that novel, Nat must murder and make love to the vanquished Margaret Whitehead. What looks finished may in fact not be ended. And the long (suppressed) nightmare of rebellion and devotion, of resistance and subservience, can only go on infuriatingly or tragically in different guises.

Such ambivalence, if this is the right word for it, often upends Styron's notions of evil. It's as if he cannot decide whether evil is some psychologically self-engendered phenomenon that may or may not be curable or whether it exists in the world as a metaphysical reality at the roots of all being. Anthony Winner describes this conundrum exactly in terms of Mason Flagg in *Set This House on Fire:*

Mr. Styron tends to define evil in terms of psychology while at the same time being unable to abandon the idea of evil as an absolute and inexplicable moral phenomenon. Psychologically, evil is defined in reference to the irrational guilts which corrode the personality and inhibit wholeness; morally, evil is postulated as man's inhumanity to man, the inexplicable desire to oppress others. Behind these two approaches to evil we find a tension between the assumptions of adjustment psychology and those of tragic humanism. . . . In Mason's case . . . we are being asked both to understand his problem (hence to view his maladjustment as the pathetic result of parental influences) *and* to judge him as evil by the absolute moral standards of tragic humanism.[37]

And the problem comes when the irrational guilt seems to overwhelm all else: causes, history, effects, whatever circumstances the character is trapped within. This guilt floats free in its corrosive darkness and taints all actions. In such a landscape evil at times remains unfocused, elusive, and hard to grasp, even though in the cases of institutionalized racial slavery and Nazi death camps, it should be more readily apparent.

What, then, happens with Styron's thematic intentions concerning human domination? If it is true, as he has admitted, that "perhaps for me life is a demonstration of oppression and submission, and variations upon them" (Morris, 36)—and we can clearly see this aspect in the relations between masters and slaves, men and women, Americans and Italians, fathers and children—and if guilt fuels all, are we to assume that domination, while an evil in and of itself, is really the great role for the guilt-ridden, self-reproaching self to play? And if not, that submission follows all too readily on its heels? If there are no God, no values, and no meaning in things, does the "typical" Styron character fantasize playing Dr. Jemand von Niemand's role in *Sophie's Choice,* sinning calculatedly and ruthlessly so as "to restore his belief in God, and at the same time to affirm his human capacity for evil, by committing the most intolerable sin that he was able to conceive? Goodness could come later. But first a great sin" (*SC,* 593). Is this the rage of an idealist caught in a world of marble and mud, or of the troublous child, having his cake and eating it too?

To authenticate the self, to try to blast it out of its self-encapsulation, Styron sets it forth on a quest, since, as he suggests, any quest is preferable to none at all. Rebellion therefore justifies itself, because to rebel is to endure, and endurance may pay off, eventually. But as Robert K. Morris and Irving Malin suggest, "Styron seldom guarantees much value beyond the self-defining act of rebellion" (Morris and Malin, 17).

We know that Styron believes in this quest, which may be his "solution" to the encapsulated self. He believes that "even in the midst of an ultimate process of dehumanization the human spirit cannot be utterly denied or downed" (*TQD,* 301). He has also said, "Perhaps I'm grounded in some manner of unconscious transcendentalism that makes me believe people really are striving for some impossible state" (Morris, 17).

In any case this striving toward some visionary unity in terms of the individual self, both destroying its former cocoon of consciousness and preserving a regenerated way of seeing with that transformed consciousness, comes out in Styron's novels in a divided manner. There are characters who observe and characters who act. In *Lie Down in Darkness* both Milton and Helen Loftis more or less observe; only Peyton acts, as all of them rebel in their own self-indulgent ways against the shrunken country-club existence masking as a particularly Virginian sense of chivalry and honor. Culver watches Mannix's revolting in his own way against the military system that Templeton stands for. Peter observes Cass, who kills Flagg, that impotent symbol of the America of the fifties, of a modern consumer society in heat. Nat devises, but Will kills, as they both oppose in their distinct manner the white slave owners and slavery itself. And Stingo listens to Sophie, who has been forced to act horrifically in her Nazi-infested past but who must pay the price of such actions. Most of the "rebels" die: Peyton and Sophie are suicides; Nat and Will are executed. Cass and Mannix manage to survive. And the observers are humanized, exorcised in some way; they "mature" in their awareness of evil and what the system can do to individuals.

From such division issues a divided result. Rebellion confronts systems of domination. These systems are shown to be evil. They have been historically created and historically determined. At the same time, the survivors— Mason and Helen Loftis, Culver, Peter and Cass, Stingo—seem merely to enter a higher stage of encapsulation. That encapsulation, however originally connected to some form of guilt or evil, has been cleansed in some way. Evil has been self-engendered and therefore can be self-eradicated, or at least consciously transcended, knowing that it will not go away completely. Perhaps Jonathan Baumbach in his description of *Set This House on Fire* is on target: "*Set This House on Fire* attempts the improbable: the alchemical transformation of impotent rage into tragic experience. Styron's rage is the hell-fire heat of the idealist faced by an unredeemably corrupt world, for which he as fallen man feels obsessively and hopelessly guilty."[38]

Does the alchemy work? Are we left with literary texts whose true focus is a kind of disconnected, autistic self that, however apparently changed, remains locked in its own vacuum? Or does Styron manage to connect these selves to a world outside them—Stingo's sexual anguish to Sophie's anguish of the soul, Cass's guilt to Mason's murder, Nat Turner's Old Testament vengeance to a very tenuous and sudden celebration of New Testament redemption? Does a "real" exorcism take place, a kind of redemption or human salvation in which the encapsulated self has been transcended and brought into the world anew? Or are these expiations forced and false? Does Styron harbor a distinctive and legitimate vision, or are we faced with a formal fictional failure in which his materials just do not bring about the kind of tragic necessity and wisdom he wants them to?

The rebellions, the oppositions, are there in all their oedipal, psychological, historical, and sexual force. The self versus society, son versus father, slave versus master, Jew versus Nazi, the self versus a vanished or malfunctioning God, the idealist versus an irremediably corrupt world, the personal versus the historical, Styron versus his southern patrimony—all these confrontations underlie Styron's work with all their social, political, psychological, epistemological, and mythical resonances. But do they remain confused and contradictory, so that the confrontation is the most that can be hoped for—to be opposed and betrayed is to be human? Or do they interact in some visionary aspect that produces a new way of seeing, an "iconic mediation" that forces us to look more deeply into ourselves as Americans in the latter part of the twentieth century, as Westerners, as people, as lost souls? These are the questions we must look at in terms of Styron's individual fictions.

One other perspective should be mentioned, and that is the Marxist notion, fashionable these days, that Styron is only functioning as a capitalist in a capitalist society, that this division in his consciousness and the encapsulated self are products of a capitalist world from which none of us can at present escape. In her extremely perceptive *Seeing and Being* (1981) Carolyn Porter argues that capitalism has always produced the reified consciousness of alienation, that in a society in which everything is reduced to the status of a commodity, what other options could possibly be open? The detached observer and the visionary seer—a division that may be one way of explaining Styron's characters—may in effect both be the alienated products of such a society and both be caught up in "a social reality breeding an extreme form of alienation." Porter suggests that we should ultimately view "the relationship between perceiving subject and perceived object as interaction rather than confrontation,"[39] and I think in many ways Styron would agree with her. Still, the confrontations, the unresolved oppositions, and the binary contradictions continue to reveal themselves, and we should examine these in the texts themselves, granting that they are the products of a capitalist world but at the same time are not the products of only that particular world.

Chapter Three
Lie Down in Darkness:
A Matter of Form

So much has been written about Styron's full-blown emergence on the literary scene in 1951 that it's difficult after all these years to try to get a new slant on his auspicious beginnings in *Lie Down in Darkness.* Styron's Faulknerian rhetoric whips up a southern miasma of sex, death, guilt, suicide, sin, and loss, all of which lies within the title of the novel, with its suggestion of fornication and fatality. Peyton Loftis's obsession with sex and flight is repeatedly described by references to lying down in darkness, a premonition of her suicide at the novel's end. And her father's loss of virginity is described in similar terms. The title takes root in its tale's dark imaginings.

In the years since the book's publication, Styron has tried to make clear what he was up to and up against. He took as his theme Poe's poetic vision, the death of a beautiful woman, which came to him in "a letter from my father in my hometown in Virginia . . . telling me of the suicide of a young girl, my age, who had been the source of my earliest and most aching infatuation. Beautiful, sweet and tortured, she had grown up in a family filled with discord and strife. I was appalled and haunted by the news of her death" (*TQD,* 290).

As with most young writers, Styron was also troubled by form and structure, by the ways to build his first novel: "The business of the progression of time seems to me one of the most difficult problems a novelist has to cope with" (Asselineau, 58). "I realized," Styron wrote in *This Quiet Dust,* "that what had been lacking in my novelist's vision was really a sense of architecture—a symmetry, perhaps unobtrusive but always there, without which a novel sprawls, becoming a self-indulged octopus" (*TQD,* 293). Styron continued:

It was a matter of form. . . . I merely had to keep aware, as I progressed with the narrative in flashback after flashback (using the funeral as a framework for the entire story) that my heroine, Peyton Loftis, would always be seen as if through the minds of the other characters; never once would I enter her consciousness. Further, she would be observed at progressive stages of her life, from childhood to early adulthood, always with certain ceremonials as a backdrop—country-club dance, a Christmas dinner, a football game, a wedding—and each of these ceremonials would not only illuminate the tensions and conflicts between Peyton and her family but provide all the atmosphere I needed to make vivid and real the upper-middle-class Virginia milieu I had set out to describe. Only at the end of the book, toward which the entire story was building—in Peyton's Molly Bloom–like monologue— would I finally enter her mind . . . suddenly and intensely "interior," and personal. (*TQD* 293–4)

Styron's problem and solution in retrospect seem both realistic and practical.

It is that form of *Lie Down in Darkness* which most intrigues us now, since it is very much a prelude to Styron's later novels. First of all, the big scenes, around which the novel swirls, each set up a celebratory rite, just as Styron intended, that is then destroyed. Confrontation upends and dramatically disrupts celebration, thus presenting in miniature the technique and rhythm of the novel as a whole. As Marc Ratner suggests, "Each scene, a small drama in itself, ends with an explosive climax" (Ratner, 42). And each scene is carefully presented in its entirety: Peyton's sixteenth birthday in 1939 at the country club, where Milton and Dolly make love in the golf museum; Christmas in 1941; the football game in Charlottesville and Maudie's final illness in November 1942; Peyton's disastrous wedding in October 1943; and Peyton's suicide and the long ride in the broken-down hearse in the heat in August 1945.

Time and Techniques

John Kenny Crane in *The Root of All Evil* ably dissects Styron's four levels of time and his construction of flashbacks, which become more intricately interwoven in the later novels but which first appear in *Lie Down in Darkness*. The transcendent present reveals the narrator telling his tale, more apparent in the up-front analyses of narrators like Cass Kinsolving, Nat Turner, and Stingo; the narrative present provides the occasion when memories are examined, as at Peyton's funeral; major flashbacks include the ceremonial confrontations described earlier; and embedded flashbacks grow out of initial flashbacks as a kind of "unexpected associative memory" (Crane, 135) that pop up during the recapitulated past. All these provide Styron's "architecture" with layers of time crisscrossing one another, creating both density and depth.

Styron applies recognizable modernist techniques to his fiction as well. We discover the stream of consciousness of Peyton's internal monologue, the discontinuities and disruptions implicit in the way minds recall events and characters, and the self-contained, resonant symbols of much modernist fiction—such as birds, clocks, children, and fathers—filled as they are with and refracted through paradoxes, ironies, and ambiguities, the "force field" of the modernist perspective. Styron even provides the appropriate waste-land setting in Potter's Field, in the marshes of Port Warwick, and in consciousness itself, "this land of rocks and shadows, walls sheering off to the depths of a soundless, stormless ocean, while far off on the heights there was a blaze without meaning, twin pyres that warned of a fear blind as dying, twin columns of smoke, a smell, a dreaming blue vapor of defilement" (*LDD,* 177). Critics have seized and recognized much of this tradition and x-rayed it accordingly.

Even imagism plays its part in *Lie Down in Darkness.* What Styron accomplishes with ceremonies he also accomplishes with images and objects. Each object is described and set within an ominous backdrop, so that each one seems profound, portentous, weighted down with a sense of doom and futility. An obvious example is a hawk, described as "a wraith, as black as smoke; the pines seemed to shake and tremble but the hawk vanished, sailing up over the roof of a filling station, a dusky shadow, wings outspread like something crucified" (*LDD,* 102). And from Milton's perspective, and the book's, "each object surrounding him . . . suggested that it was not *he* who existed at all: he was the inanimate one . . . and these . . . were possessed of thriving, noisy life and the power to drive one witless with anxiety" (*LDD,* 144). In effect Styron's palpable universe often seems to contain more ominous life than the characters themselves.

Robert Dale Parker in describing what he calls Faulkner's "novelistic imagination" explores Faulkner's use of repression in his texts, that sequence of withholding information and secrets which creates expectation in the reader and involves him or her in the unveiling of the sequence itself. Such repression, akin to puritanical confessions, simultaneously blocks and demands revelation, making the revelation at once worse and necessary, an experience "in which the intensity of secret sin only increases the urge to pry into and expose it."[1]

This essentially Gothic "architecture" describes Styron's methods as well as it does Faulkner's: "And if modernism . . . heralded the demise of plot in favor of consciousness and technical virtuosity, then Faulkner took ʳhe same techniques he learned from modernism and, applying them with melodramatic selectivity, joined them to the new taking for granted of Freud, to the gothic, to romance and to the nineteenth-century American romance-novel tradition. . . . The origin of novels built around momentous mysteries and appalling absences . . . is itself peculiarly modern" (Parker, 12–13). Peyton's monologue and suicide fit comfortably in such a description.

The effects of this form may be the real triumph of *Lie Down in Darkness*. Time and consciousness appear weighted, thick, coiled, and circuitous. They even share the incestuousness of time's feeding upon itself in the characters' consciousness, a parallel to the incestuous feelings Milton has for his daughter Peyton. In such a way the form dramatizes and makes palpable a significant theme of the novel. Space becomes claustrophobic in such circumstances, for characters feel trapped and imprisoned by memories and one another. In such a realm the Loftis family itself becomes a claustrophobic cell. Richard Gray describes that "powerful sense of reenactment attaching itself to almost every thought and gesture—all this makes us feel that the dark backward and abysm of the old world lies just below the surface of landscape and consciousness, waiting for an appropriate moment to reappear." And thus characters seem like creatures from Poe's tales, "like a somnambulist driven by forces beyond one's personal control, distilling within the blood the inherited obsessions of an entire race" (R. Gray, 287).

"Cocooned" Characters

All the characters are cocooned in such conscious architecture. They are implicated with one another, caught in the web of one another's failings, feelings, and circumstances. They remain permanently compromised and "doomed." In one way Peyton's suicide seems a triumph, in that she ejects herself from this cocoon. The novel is built on recurrent and resonant motifs and moods, in that kind of weighted consciousness which perpetuates itself and its grief but offers no solution or escape. Sir Thomas Browne's quotation at the beginning of the story declares that "diurnity is a dream and folly of expectation" because of the reality of "the brother of death." In such a context Peyton's suicide in recognizing that dark brotherhood at least takes an almost "positive" stand in choosing to lie down in darkness permanently rather than in the dark, coiling consciousness the other characters haven't the courage to shed.

This web of consciousness undermines any attempt to get to the heart of things, since in this novel such a consciousness *is* the heart of things. When Carey Carr asks himself who was to blame in the self-destruction of the Loftis family, he gets nowhere: "Mad or not, Helen had been beastly. . . . Yet Loftis himself had been no choice soul; and who, finally, lest it be God himself, could know where the circle, composed as it was of such tragic suspicions and misunderstandings, began, and where it ended? Who was the author of the original misdeed?" (*LDD,* 228). In many ways Styron's architecture has authored the deed; the formal and intricate web of time and consciousness, as constructed here, has produced the sense of doom and futility. It may be that place where characters exist "only to be drawn back always by some force [they] could never define" (*LDD,* 254). The novel's success and power may rest in its form and style.

Conceptually or thematically, the book stands on less certain ground. True, *Lie Down in Darkness* is a study of "a very modern, hedonistic segment of urban rich society living without faith and purpose" (Rubin, 65), and social dissolution dogs its every step. There is a social milieu or veneer presented here in the web and woof of Styron's ceremonies. We get what Albert Berger in the novel refers to as a very southern "*husk* of culture . . . with its cancerous religiosity, its exhausting need to put manners before morals, to negate all ethos" (*LDD,* 346). This element is as much implicit in the ceremonial setups with which the novel has been constructed as it is in the theme of social dissolution. There is a decided modern-day, Episcopal Virginia culture, one in which "all real Virginia gentlemen . . . put safely behind [them] tragic thoughts and tragic events" (*LDD,* 244), and Episcopalians, "nominally, at least, [are] not inclined by conscience to worry long over abstractions" (*LDD,* 11). It is a culture in which Dolly can "[listen] not so much to the substance of what [Milton] said as to the tone of the words, the melodious, really endearing way he said them" (*LDD,* 66), and in which wedding guests admire the "soft and sweet, insidiously compelling" voice of Carey Carr, since Episcopalians "are often partial to the home and always partial to the poetic quality of their service" (*LDD,* 257, 256).

Styron's melodious South, outside of Port Warwick, is "a land of prim pastoral fences, virgin timber, grazing sheep and Anglo-Saxons. . . . Many were Episcopalians, and all prayed and hunted quail with equal fervor. . . . Destiny had given them a peaceful and unvanquished land to live in, free of railroads and big-city ways . . . and when they died they died, for the most part, in contentment, shriven of their moderate, parochial sins. . . . They lived in harmony with nature and called themselves the last Americans" (*LDD,* 215). That sense of peace and contentment, while ostensibly the superficial qualities Styron's darker imaginings are breaking through, also seem to bolster the web of consciousness in the novel, as if "doom" were just one more thing to relish "with equal fervor."

Richard Gray here raises the question, "When the old institutions become irrelevant and the old myths obsolete, *and when our habits of thought and feeling continue nevertheless to be shaped by them*—how then do we change the situation?" Styron, Gray maintains, offers no change but remains caught up in the Loftises's problems, as much as he "depends . . . on the earlier *literary* tradition of the South just as Milton, Helen, and Peyton Loftis all depend on its broader cultural tradition" (R. Gray, 288–89).

This dependence on literary tradition shows up in Styron's characters. The power of his landscape and atmosphere asserts itself almost independently of these more stereotypical characters, as he himself has acknowledged, in "the story's rich possibilities—the weather and the landscape of Tidewater, *against which* the characters began to define themselves: father, mother, sister, and the girl herself, all doomed by fatal hostility and misunderstanding, all *helpless victims* of a domestic tragedy. In writing such a story—like Flaubert in *Madame Bovary,* which I passionately admired—I would also be able to anatomize bourgeois family life of the kind that I knew so well, the WASP world of the modern urban South [italics mine]" (*TQD,* 291). In the novel the characters are described accurately as "this breed of monsters" (*LDD,* 227) and as "a family of warriors" (268), but the ultimate accolade may be Styron's own, jotted down in the margin of his manuscript: "These people give me the creeps" (Ruderman, 49).

The Loftises within the architecture of the novel appear one-dimensional and thin. Richard Gray goes so far as to see them as parodies of themselves: Milton as "a comic travesty of the traditional Southern gentleman," Helen as "a parody of the Southern lady, her fragility and gentleness all dissolved into neuroticism," and Peyton as "a brutal parody of the Southern belle" (R. Gray, 288). In this he is fairly close to the mark. Need we rehearse once again Milton's self-indulgent, childish despair and faith, riding on booze and incestuous longings and relying on his "sophomoric fatalism" to get him through; or Helen's self-righteous Puritan-romantic notions of sin and her sanctimonious inability to forgive; or Peyton's spoiled, explosive rages and sexual misadventures? Carey Carr represents the cultural husk, the minister-as-therapist whose belief in God is as foggy and uncertain as everybody else's. The blacks in their religious murmurings; Harry Miller, the Jewish artist; and Dolly, the fatuous mistress appear almost as stick figures to fill roles rather than as full-blooded souls in their own "rite."

Freudian Fathers

As several critics have pointed out, the popular Freudianism of the fifties, in particular the knowledge of the oedipal complex, has eaten away at the fabric of society and at consciousness itself. Virginia is appropriately de-

scribed as the "Cradle of the Nation" (*LDD*, 303). Flannery O'Connor may
have said it best: "To my way of thinking [*Lie Down in Darkness*] was too
much the long tedious Freudian case history, though the boy can write and
there were overtones of better things in it."[2] And Marc Ratner describes the
characters as creatures trapped in a "Freudian determinism which rarely
frees [them] to go beyond the stages of childhood or adolescence in their
search for identity" (Ratner, 54).

The clue lies in the novel's second epigraph from *Finnegans Wake:* "Carry
me along, taddy, like you done through the toy fair." The characters seem to
rely on and despise their fathers, often deriding them, often clinging to
them, as if in doing so they need not take any responsibility for their own
wasted lives. The pretentious pronouncements of Milton's father, "a lawyer,
descended from a long line of lawyers" (*LDD*, 12), often echo in his son's
memory, full of words like "good judgment . . . ideals inherent . . . especially in Virginians, [and] relics of vanquished grandeur" (*LDD*, 13, 44,
174). The father, who spoiled his son, speaks in epigrams: "We are the
driblet turds of angels, not men but a race of toads" (*LDD*, 174); *"Only
poets and thieves can exercise free will, and most of them die young. . . . Suffer
in your hot desire then perhaps you will understand, patience, my son"* (*LDD*,
91, 151). Such lines continue to haunt Milton, though he recognizes that
"Papa could never realize that such talk was meant only for those who had
no dilemmas anyway," that he was "an old man in whom obscurity resembled solemnity often enough, and solemnity wisdom," and that "when he
was alive I hated him. Now he's gone. That's all I can say" (*LDD*, 151, 41,
175). Loss is so much a part of Milton's sensibilities that only when something has been lost can it be truly meaningful.

The fathers march on, striking their outmoded poses and fear into the
hearts of their children. Helen is the true daughter of "Blood and Jesus
Peyton": " 'Helen,' he'd say, 'Helen, sweetheart. We must stand fast with
the good' . . . and I thought he was just like God" (*LDD*, 107). Peyton, of
course, has Milton, stuck in the syrupy solution of guilt, incest, and parental
smothering. Even for more or less normal and unexceptional Dick
Cartwright—who later turns out to be impotent in Peyton's arms, emblematic of the lot of all of them, perhaps—"his father baffled him, and as a
child Dick was torn between love and hatred. . . . It is inevitable that men
with such ambivalent natures should have strange effects on their sons"
(*LDD*, 216).

Ella's and La Ruth's faith in Daddy Faith, the black evangelist, serves as
an ironic contrast to the whites' incestuous grip, for however much of a
showman and humbug that Faith is, his converts see their salvation in him

and manage to offer up a kind of hallelujah at the novel's end in the presence of "the oncoming night."

The leap from father to God is not difficult. In a godless world, the fathers have fled, but they seem to have left nothing in their place except outmoded, corroded devotions and despair. God the father in this novel reveals obvious Freudian raiments, no more so than when Helen declares to Carey Carr, "Your God is a silly old ass . . . and my God . . . my God is the devil!" (*LDD*, 286). Evil becomes the obsessive plaything of the spoiled child, a projection on the world of failed hopes and narcissistic ambitions. Carey Carr has it right: "What he [Carr] knew of psychology had led him to believe that too powerful a consciousness of evil was often the result of infantile emotions: hence primitive fundamentalism, especially the American brand. . . . The cowardly Puritan . . . unwilling to partake of free religious inquiry, uses the devil as a scapegoat to rid himself of the need for positive action: 'The devil *forced* me,' he says" (*LDD*, 113). And is it no wonder, then, that Styron's visions of damnation in the novel affect children, "those combustible infants plunged to hell, who stretched out their tiny arms to a pitiless, fiend-faced Abraham and shrieked eternal baby cries of agony and burning" (*LDD*, 217)? In bed together Peyton and Dick Cartwright "were painted with fire, like those fallen children who live and breathe and soundlessly scream, and whose souls blaze forever" (*LDD*, 225).

What is at the center of "their peculiarly modern despair" (*LDD*, 223)? There are lots of tag lines but little essence. We get drowning, drifting, "vague amorphous sorrows" (*LDD*, 103), time and remembrance, a fundamentalist doom, the dead end of exhausted emotions that comes across as an enervating nostalgia, and loss, all of which seem self-justifying explanations, abstractions to blame one's dissolution on someone or something else. "Most kids these days are not wrong or wrongdoers," Peyton tells her Bunny. "They're just aimless and lost, more aimless than you all ever thought of being" (*LDD*, 255). "Those people back in the Lost Generation," Peyton explains, "they weren't lost. What they were doing was losing us" (*LDD*, 224). At times Styron can rise to express the loss of an idealist trapped in a corrupt and corrupting world in his description of "Mozart, a song of measureless innocence that echoed among lost ruined temples of peace and brought to their dreams an impossible vision: of a love that outlasted time and dwelt even in the night, beyond reach of death and all the immemorial, descending dusks" (*LDD*, 225). But for the most part Styron seems as much at sea in this emotional, self-indulgent labyrinth as his characters.

"Guilt is the thing with feathers" (*LDD*, 335), bemoans Peyton, negating Emily Dickinson's notions about hope. And the novel thrives on guilts of all kinds, from "Freudian attachments" to the seemingly metaphysical agony, "like the soul that forever seeks a grace, upon his own particular guilt" (*LDD,* 59), from the "soul-disease" (*LDD,* 144) that seems to eat away at Milton's very being to the South itself, where "the ground is bloody and full of guilt" (*LDD,* 69).

From a positive position this amorphous emotional center, ripe with melancholy moods and notions of exile, has been described as a great achievement by Elizabeth Janeway, who locates Styron's triumph in his ability "to plumb private emotion as it is felt privately in obscure half-articulate symbols and to communicate the weight of this emotion to the reader. . . . It is a search for meaning."[3] Howard Mumford Jones described *Lie Down in Darkness* as a very moralist vision, picturing "a set of people living without God in the world."[4] And Jan B. Gordon sees it as "practically a concordance of southern puritanism. . . . *Lie Down in Darkness* has all the trappings of one of the ancient fertility myths, with everyone asking the same question, namely what will restore fertility to the kingdom of sterility" (Gordon, 115, 118), a kind of southern Eliotic wasteland.

But Jonathan Baumbach may be closer to the truth in his sense that the novel fails "to achieve focus" (Baumbach, 24). As Harvey Breit summed it up: "It starts out as a bleak and black book and it ends as one; there is no catalyst here."[5] In effect the center will not hold, though the architecture around it is splendid.

In describing Hawthorne as a romancer, Michael Davitt Bell explored Hawthorne's vision of revealing how impulse and spirit became all too easily entangled in dead forms and mere rhetoric, how the revolutionary Puritan spirit of early America slipped all too quickly "into the verbal mask, the rhetoric, of nineteenth-century culture." "The legacy of Puritanism," Bell concludes from Hawthorne's vision, "was a world of hollow abstractions, shells of spirit—a world of words." Styron's abstractions, his mellifluous rhetoric, and the time-structured architecture of *Lie Down in Darkness* give, finally, the weight and sense of doom to the novel more than the characters and the story within which he has cocooned them. He may in effect be paralleling Hawthorne's—or Faulkner's—own presentation of "the descent from momentary inspiration to repressive formalism as an inevitable psychological and historical process."[6] In any case that descent has begun long before the novel begins, and the repressive formalism of Styron's southern landscape and the structure of the book both pass for the moral decay, the "search for meaning," which they don't so much reveal and explore as embalm.

Perhaps Styron's intentions paralleled the Jewish artist Harry Miller's, Peyton's ill-fated husband, who laments, "Call me a disillusioned innocent, a renegade Red, or whatever, I want to crush in my hands all that agony and make beauty come out, because that's all that's left, and I don't have much time" (*LDD,* 360). And there are brilliant, resonant moments in this long, ponderous first novel, products perhaps of Styron's way of writing, his attention to language, the slow polishing of his separate episodes.

But it is the architecture that remains the triumph today. And perhaps, in writing about the writing of *Lie Down in Darkness,* much later, Styron knew it:

And so then, after I had completed the first forty pages or so (all of which I was satisfied with and which remain intact in the final version), there began a wrestling match between myself and my own demon—which is to say, that part of my literary consciousness which too often has let me be indolent and imitative, false to my true vision of reality, responsive to facile echoes rather than the inner voice. . . . I had to deafen myself to echoes of Scott Fitzgerald, always so easy and seductive, rid my syntax of the sonorities of Conrad and Thomas Wolfe [and Faulkner, who is, of course, both the god and the demon of all southern writers who followed him], cut out wayward moments of Hemingway attitudinizing, above all, be myself. . . . I found the quest incredibly difficult . . . and so, after a fine start—I quit. (*TQD,* 292)

He quit writing but was then rescued by architecture, the way to restructure time to fit his vision. The theme of that vision in *Lie Down in Darkness* at best remains murky, but its presentation in form and language, however overwrought in places, remains the novel's true triumph. Styron's first novel left him in search of a theme, yet it also left him with the nearly fully mature techniques and devices with which to deal with that theme once he could find it.

Chapter Four
The Long March:
A Failed Rebellion

Of *Lie Down in Darkness* Styron once told David Dempsey, "I wanted to tell the story of four tragically fated people, one of them [Maudie] the innocent victim of the others. It was important to me that I write about this thing, but I can't tell you why . . . to me the important thing was the story" (Hoffman, 152). If the "thing" seemed to elude Styron in his recollection of writing his first novel, it did not do so in writing his second. Rebellion is the motivating force in *The Long March*. At least one of his characters had chosen to stand up rather than lie down. And rebellion by its very nature suggests a shattering of the cocoon within which the encapsulated Loftises found themselves.

The Long March also stands as the prototype for several of Styron's later longer novels. Besides the thrust and crisis of rebellion on which the book is based, we also find the bifurcated hero, the observant witness, and the participant rebel, what David L. Minter has described in American literature as the distinction between the man of interpretation and the man of action or design. Such dialectical characters include Ishmael and Ahab in *Moby-Dick*, Nick Carraway and Jay Gatsby in *The Great Gatsby*, Coverdale and Hollingsworth in Hawthorne's *The Blithedale Romance*, and more recently Quention Compson and Thomas Sutpen in Faulkner's *Absalom, Absalom!*[1]

The Long March also looks more closely at the individual's relationship with society, at the familiar oedpial struggles of the first novel, at the kind of Manichaean mysteries involving the confrontational polarities and unresolved oppositions in the book, and at Styron's own attempts to come to some metaphysical vision that can encompass all these many attributes and perspectives.

Suffering and Rebellion

At the core of *The Long March* lies Styron's description of the suffering that human beings must endure. This suffering seems to be at the heart of the human condition as Styron views it through less southern-nostalgic eyes than in *Lie Down in Darkness*. Life becomes a long march, full of accident, anxiety, dread, exhaustion, pride, loneliness, and panic, filling the individual with a sense of outrage and violation, locked into some robotized routine. In short, life becomes a war in and of itself. "War was no longer simply a temporary madness into which human beings happily lapsed from time to time," Styron commented in 1963. "War had at last become *the* human condition" ("Afterword," 71).

Suffering provides the underlying motif of *The Long March*. And Mannix, the Jew from Brooklyn, becomes the emblem of "one of tortured and gigantic suffering."[2] Such suffering may be part of the hero's role, and if so Mannix would certainly fill that category. And yet since Colonel Templeton firmly believes that "the hike had had nothing to do with courage or sacrifice or suffering" (*LM*, 117), Styron undermines this simplistic heroic notion and leaves to the reader the task of interpreting for himself or herself the ultimate significance of suffering.

Traditional liberal values would place much of the meaning of existence upon the individual consciousness, no matter how terrible conditions had become around it. Essentially, this idea has been the key to Western tragedy as a genre and vision. And yet like suffering, the worth of the individual in *The Long March* is not taken for granted. For one thing, in Styron's novel individuals can be reduced to mere functions, men to marines, and become conformist, resigned, and even absurd when viewed as mere cogs in a wheel. And from this perspective individual rebellion or protest embodies only the absurd, since such protest can make the individual's situation not only worse but also self-victimizing and, in the end, existentially absurd: "Born into a generation of conformists, even Mannix (so Culver sensed) was aware that his gestures were not symbolic, but individual, therefore hopeless, maybe even absurd, and that he was trapped like all of them in a predicament which one personal insurrection could, if anything, only make worse" (*LM*, 61).

This predicament leaves Styron's wondering about the very nature of Mannix's rebellion against Colonel Templeton's rule: "He only mutilated himself by this perverse and violent rebellion" (*LM*, 107). If Mannix rebels, as he does, by willfully submitting to Templeton's long march, a kind of "rebellion in reverse" (*LM*, 79), then isn't he in effect only proving how pervasive the system really is? If the self has been so corrupted by the system that it can view itself only as a function of that system, and if its way to rebel or to conform in effect proves the same thing, then doesn't Mannix's revolt only prove that without the system, there is no self? And if this is true, then the individual self is a liberal myth that no longer exists, and any individual action, of which there can be no real example, is doomed to meaninglessness and absurdity. But if this is Styron's case, then "individual" rebellion in *The Long March* has only reinforced what we've already experienced in *Lie Down in Darkness:* the modern encapsulated self is cocooned in so pervasive a system of social and cultural regulations that Styron's true subject is that web and its continued insidious power in trapping us—and perhaps our hopeless but nostalgic desire to escape and live without it.

Styron sets up his regulars carefully. Each acts his function as a marine, even if it seems to go against his basic instincts as a man. O'Leary believes that all are "inextricably grafted to the system" and should display "a devoted, methodical competence" despite what doubts the person might have (*LM*, 29). Bill Lawrence symbolizes the clean-cut, spoiled, and arrogant functionary in the system. And Culver even begins to think that O'Leary may be right and Mannix hopelessly, willfully wrong.

Colonel Templeton, with his set of fixed attitudes and habitualized gestures, embodies the system perfectly: "He had too long been conditioned by the system to perform with grace a human act" (*LM*, 95). For him every action to be performed is a task, not a personal action involving moral value. He is as devoted as a priest to his religious rites, "almost benevolent . . . [one] in whom passion and faith had made an alloy. . . . Above meanness or petty spite, he was leading a march to some humorless salvation" (*LM*, 93).

And of course Templeton is a father figure to his men, the man with the responsibility, half-feared, half-worshiped, but ultimately never really questioned. His men acquiesce to "the voice that commanded, once again, *you will*," for after all they seem to be as "helpless as children," and "they were only marines, responding anew to the old commands" (*LM*, 75 6). This "stern father" (*LM*, 89) is someone to both hate and placate. He sets the rules, and his "children" follow or disobey them, but they never question his godlike role. "Culver almost liked the Colonel, in some negative way . . . 'respect' . . . was the nearest approach" (*LM*, 36). "He's not a bad guy . . . just a regular," Culver explains, reducing the father to a function and letting that function circumscribe and conjure up a world in which to function.

Styron's vision becomes confusing here. If the "old-fashioned" sense of seeing things on an individual basis—good verses evil, good guy verses bad guy—is itself absurd, because the system recognizes only functions and effects, and if in his reverse rebellion Mannix proves himself to be just a better player at Templeton's own game, then doesn't the characters'— and Styron's—"outrage . . . at the system, at their helpless plight, the state of the world" (*LM*, 38) seem forced and absurd, too? Is this "real" outrage, voiced by an individual consciousness, or merely the necessary oil in the gears of functionaries going about their business and preserving the system no matter what? Can suffering be made symbolic of some larger metaphysical distress built into the human or a universal condition, or is it merely a physical given, like the necessity to eat and sleep? Is Styron himself stranded between the romantic notion of the individual's attacking the system in order to stand up for superior moral rights or reasons and the more "existential" condition of suffering as a given, with no symbolic resonance whatsoever?

In the workings out of this dilemma in *The Long March,* Styron tries to achieve a more coherently symbolic significance. Culver and Mannix, however different temperamentally, after all do not remain static. They change and develop, separately and in relation to each other. And yet they are in many ways polarized, a structural phenomenon of the novel that may be built on Styron's own dialectical or bifurcated view of systematic authority and individual conscience, complicated by the oedipal tensions we have already recognized.

The question may finally be whether or not Styron resents authority in and of itself or resents an attitude that some figures in authority exhibit. In any case in *The Long March,* as a prelude to his later novels, the polarity of vision seems to lie at the heart of the matter and helps to explain the fabric of unresolved confrontations in the novel.

Culver's Confusions

Tom Culver shows all the symptoms of a contented, domesticated civilian suddenly thrust back into war. He comes to realize that all may be "astray at mid-century in the never-endingness of war" (*LM,* 124) and that this atmosphere may account for his sense of anxiety, dread, solitude, and fear, and yet he is understandably at first shocked by his recall. After World War II he enjoys the civilian refuge of children, home, and classical music and fills his sweet thoughts with reveries of "two little girls playing on the sunny grass" (*LM,* 65). His enforced return to military uniform fills him with resentment and dread, and he feels suddenly imprisoned in a nightmare realm of permanent disruption, adrift in the hypnagogic state "like the dream of a man delirious with fever . . . enclosed within the tent, unmoored and unhelmed upon a dark and compassless ocean" (*LM,* 41). He suddenly views his new world "as if . . . through drug-glazed eyes" (*LM,* 67). Displaced, uprooted, and "profoundly alone," Culver epitomizes the ordinary man trapped in a century of war.

Al Mannix is at first far more vocally disgruntled than Culver. He seems bitter, sardonic, and frank and in taking things personally despises Templeton almost on sight. He refuses to answer a colonel's questions during a lecture and decides to walk the thirty-six miles of the enforced march despite the nail in his heel. To beat the system, he feels, one must *be* the system, and Culver warily watches his transformation into a fanatic, a kind of supraorthodox heretic in the religious ranks, an absolutist bully obsessed with his own demonstration of rebellion, whatever the ultimate import. To Mannix, Templeton becomes "a prime and calculated evil" (*LM*, 45) against which he (Mannix) will fight in his own way. And very quickly "the contagion of Mannix's fear had touched [Culver]" (*LM*, 44).

Significant differences proliferate between Culver and Mannix as Styron develops their characters. And in these escalating differences Styron seems to be building his polarized vision of rebellion and authority. Mannix faces death when dangled from a hotel window in San Francisco, while Culver grapples with his anxiety when faced with Mannix. When the explosion occurs and marines are killed, Culver throws up at the scene, while Mannix weeps and sees it as symbolizing a greater evil: "Won't they ever let us alone?" (*LM*, 69). To Mannix, Templeton is evil incarnate; to Culver, a more or less blameless functionary and, however vaguely, a demonic father figure. At one point Culver stops Mannix in his rebellion, as if the more resigned conformist were tackling the outspoken if necessarily doomed rebel—"That's enough, Al!"—but he cries as he does it and feels his own spirit as it "sank like a rock" (*LM*, 112–13).

Culver's confusion about the meaning of events is met and transcended by Mannix's certainty. Mannix seems to represent a tragic endurance that will continue against all odds. And despite the absurdity of Mannix's rebellion, Styron seems to want us to see an aura of Christian, classical, and humanist values hovering around that character's actions. And yet Culver's confusion proves to be far more human eventually, since he quickly sees how bullying and fanatic Mannix has become. Perhaps only victimhood is ensured when Mannix is confronted naked by the black maid at the end of the novel, as if, as each relates to the other on the basic human level of sympathy and pain, both are recognizing their roles as victims in the larger society and system.

Styron's vision may emerge more clearly in *The Long March* because he tackles his theme of rebellion and his uncertain attitude toward it more diagrammatically than in *Lie Down in Darkness*. As he himself has explained, "I wanted to free myself from Faulkner's influence before starting another full-scale book. *The Long March* was my disintoxication exercise"

(Coindreau, 104). As noted previously, he has described himself as a "provisional rebel" (Coale), and that self-description certainly seems justified when seen in relation to the polarities on which *The Long March* has been built.

The Structure of the March

Styron's second novel displays endless confrontations and juxtapositions. Chronological time from noon to noon confronts the nightmarish, hypnagogic state of dreams and anxieties. Culver's dream encompasses the night before the long march, with its tales of Mannix's past, culminating in his facing death in San Francisco. At twilight the marines start off on their trek. By 4:15 A.M. they are eighteen miles into the march, halfway to the finish line. And at noon they have arrived at Heaven's Gate, an apotheosis of sorts. The opening scene of horror reverberates throughout the entire tale, mesmerizing Culver and shaking and finally transforming Mannix. Culver experiences his three reveries involving young girls and music, the nostalgia of home and youth.

Styron arranges three friezes in the novel, two between Templeton and Mannix and one final one between Mannix and the black maid. The first emphasizes "classical Greek masks, made of chrome or tin, reflecting an almost theatrical disharmony" (*LM*, 35) between the two marines, when they are viewed in Culver's mind as opposites in a dynamic tension, as polarities set up for eternal conflict: master and slave. The second frieze presents them as "twin profiles embattled" (*LM*, 116), just before Mannix is court-martialed. The polarities hold, but they are now twin polarities, fellow marines upholding the same system. And the final frieze, realized on a more human scale, presents Mannix and the maid as "communicating . . . sympathy and understanding" (*LM*, 126), both victims and slaves of the system that rules their lives. Styron employs throughout his images of classical tragedy and Egyptian slavery as a way of highlighting these basic confrontations.

Polarities also appear on a more thematic level. They permeate the novel like Manichaean mysteries, "Manichaean" in the sense of a pervasive, unresolved dualism, forever entangled and at war with one another, as opposed to the more orthodox Christian sense of unity and deliverance from battle. Sunshine opposes darkness, sound confronts silence, heat undermines the cold. Disruptions threaten chronological sequence and consciousness, just as Styron confronts peace with war, Heaven's Gate with prison, submission with rebellion, and Culver's reveries of classical music and sanctuary with life itself.

At times these contradictions temporarily dissolve into a kind of hypnagogic state, in which all moral categories collapse, nightmare takes over, and
anything is possible. With Styron's descriptions of wails in hell in the
swamp; of dark seas, spooky glows, and the green light of dawn; of the marines as zombies, ghosts, wraiths, and robots; and of night as one long
nightmare of pain and exhaustion, which in Culver "enveloped his whole
spirit" (*LM*, 98), the novel seems to enter the disturbingly sentient universe
of a Poe tale, and all morally symbolic structures or images that try to embody individual rebellion and the system nearly vanish. "Korea . . . the very
idea of another war . . . possessed a kind of murky, surrealistic, half-lunatic
unreality that we are mercifully spared while awake, but which we do occa-
sionally confront in a horrible dream," wrote Styron in his introduction to
the Norwegian edition of *The Long March*. "With the reality of some unshakable nightmare . . . in the summer of 1952, I found myself in Paris still
unable to shake off the sense of having just recently awakened from a nightmare" (*TQD*, 300).

And yet even in such a clearheaded, short novel as *The Long March*,
Styron has still managed to blur the significance of his tale. If it is a Gothic
nightmare, then the "existential-romantic" tangle of self and society is su-
perseded. If it is a morality tale with Gothic trappings, then can it both celebrate the individual and define him only in terms that show him to be
merely a function in the larger military-social scheme of things? Is there a
thin line between genuine polarities and contradictions, which seem to be at
the center of Styron's vision here, and mere metaphysical confusion? Do the
oedipal overtones undermine or further explain Culver's and Mannix's actions and beings?

Critics remain divided on these issues. Marc Ratner maintains that "for
Styron the great value of action is that, through rebellion, the rebel discovers
the evils of the 'System' in himself, cuts through his self-illusions, and exor-
cises his devils to become a mature person" (Ratner, 69). But what are we to
make of a maturity that leaves a brutal system intact with no real questions
asked? Is this maturity or an evasion of the very issues the author seems to
be raising? Even tone may be an issue here, as Roger Asselineau suggests:
"The satirical tone of many a passage is thus neutralized by the understanding of the futile nature of revolt" (Asselineau, 94).

Irving Malin mounts a very strong case for Culver as a "solitary observer,"
as a man who "lies between his superiors, between all the opposites of life.
He dangles." To Malin, Culver is trapped both by the marines and by his
own body. He "regards himself as an actor in someone else's script" and continues to see visions that, "like Styron's symbolic details, are full of commin-

gled opposites." In the end "Culver feels a 'deep vast hunger' for some transcendental vision which will overarch grottolike peace and threatening storm . . . His hunger dies. He must live with the 'hateful contraries' . . . with war and peace."[3] Culver, in effect, accepts the book's polarized view of things, which may be essentially Styron's own in 1952. And in doing so, Culver in effect changes nothing. Nothing has been so much learned as accepted.

In Culver's acceptance, however, one can't help but feel that whatever rebellious outbreak has been possible at the beginning of the novel, by the end it has fizzled out. *The Long March* may leave us as encapsulated as did *Lie Down in Darkness,* wherein even the exercise of outright rebellion only proves the existence of the walls of the prison cell, and however held up by vaunted polarities and dualistic designs, the cell remains intact. As Norman Kelvin has suggested, "We find opposites striving for union through conflict or love . . . in which heightened awareness, or an intensification of the spiritual, is attempted but unattained" (Kelvin, 208). We will subsequently explore this observation in detail.

Culver and Styron seem to be straining for a vision that can unite opposites. But with the seeming acceptance of an institutionalized system with man's place faithfully circumscribed within it, the straining can seem only like carping, whining about and against what the novelist has already accepted as unalterable fact. As one critic has explained, "Styron creates his personae's visions from metaphors of reality. His characters' yearning for the 'impossible state,' for (in their terms) a finer, more desirable world, even for some glorious surceases from the anxieties and pressures of this one, are always built upon what is concrete, mundane, ordinary: as though their symbolic imagination need root itself in the solid stuff of life" (Morris and Malin, 4). That may be an inevitable human condition, but it does bring to mind Styron's more or less contented Episcopalians living contentedly with nature and their Virginian world in *Lie Down in Darkness.* Such ultimate feelings of ease in the world may dampen any rebellious quests and render them stillborn.

Nevertheless, *The Long March* lays out in fairly simple detail the developing scope of Styron's vision, stripped as it is of the organ-toned, Faulknerian presence of *Lie Down in Darkness.* Initially the second novel seems to indicate a breakthrough, a leap beyond lying to standing up. But at the last it remains curiously locked within that essentially polarized and encapsulated vision not yet jettisoned or overcome. The unresolved Manichaean mysteries are presented in all their dualistic elegance, but the nature of rebellion, individual consciousness, and society and the interactions of all of them remain blurred and confusing, if not confused. What better way to get out of this visionary bind than to set the whole house on fire and thrust a burning soul into the midst of it to see what it's really made of? That seemed to be Styron's next objective in his grappling with his own paradoxical and increasingly polarized vision.

Chapter Five

Set This House on Fire: A Puddle of Self

"Ravello was one giant house party,"[1] wrote biographer Gerald Clarke in describing the making of the movie *Beat the Devil,* with director John Huston; actors Humphrey Bogart, Gina Lollobrigida, Jennifer Jones, Peter Lorre, and Robert Morley; and the screenwriter who had been called in, Truman Capote. Into this scene wandered William and Rose Styron, just married in Rome in May 1953. They stayed for more than a year, before buying a house in Connecticut. "I had an awe of those people almost teenage in its dazzlement," Peter Leverett was to say about the movie colony in *Set This House on Fire* (*SHF,* 60).

But Leverett was also to describe himself in somewhat darker terms: "Estranged from myself and from my time, dwelling neither in the destroyed past nor in the fantastic and incomprehensible present, I knew that I must find the answer to at least several things" (*SHF,* 19). Styron described himself at that time as undergoing a "kind of chaotic wandering that I was enduring" (talk at RWC).

In *Set This House on Fire*—the book that was to receive such negative American reviews but such laudatory French reviews and that was to be remaindered in the United States within a year of its publication—Styron combined the architecture of *Lie Down in Darkness* with the themes of *The Long March.* The emblematic and dramatic confrontational scenes, the flashbacks-within-flashbacks, the layered time sequences and recapitulations he employed along with the themes of rebellion, of the individual and society, complete with elaborate notions of guilt, oedipal tensions, and the reality and horror of suffering. All the Gothic-romantic structure and perspectives are here, filled with dreams of doom and the rhetoric to match.

The novel reads like a massively energized self-purgation, an exorcism or self-conflagration, as if the author were publicly immolating himself and his fictional world to clear the landscape and start anew. At the same time, that purgation reveals once again encapsulated selves claustrophobically cocooned in their own loud harangues and self-indulgent outrages. The same queasy and unresolved relationship between rebellion, the individual, and society that was present in *The Long March* is here inflated by the Faulknerian rhetoric that seems to be the driving force, the primal howl behind it. Needless to say, the results appear to be more mixed and uncertain than in the first two novels.

The Murder

The story unwinds like a murder mystery or gothic romance, as it both approaches and flees from the facts of Mason Flagg's murder. The French may have been drawn to it for these very reasons, since, as Melvin J. Friedman suggests, the novel does have much in common with the French *nouveau roman* of the time, as "a mock-detective novel with mythic parallels."[2] And the focus moves inexorably from the outer ring of consciousness—Peter Leverett as lawyerlike observer, who shares some of Cass Kinsolving's angst—into the center of the maelstrom in Cass's being, from part-knowledge to the whole truth, from speculation to the revelation of Cass's murder of Flagg and Cass's redemption at the hands of Luigi, the fascist-humanist policeman in Sambuco.

Peter gives us Mason Flagg as a spoiled rich boy at prep school, as a married philanderer in New York, and as the rich interloper in Sambuco. The reader gets glimpses of the final fatal night in Sambuco, of death and a Hollywood party, a threatening note from Cass to Mason, Cass's degrading performance for Mason as ringmaster at the party. In the present Peter meets Cass in South Carolina, and on a boat in the Ashley River, Cass confesses to his murdering Mason, to his alcoholic fits in Paris, to his impotent art, and to the loss of his virginity to the Jehovah's Witness, Vernelle Satterfield. In May, Mason comes to Sambuco, to which Cass, his wife, Poppy, and their innumerable children have already come, and mistaking Cass for a famous hermetic painter soon seduces him with his PX connections to liquor.

Luigi, the policeman in Sambuco, sets up Francesca to help at Cass's villa. Her father, Michele, has tuberculosis and a broken leg, and she and Cass steal food from Mason to help him. Francesca comes to work for Mason, and as part of his manipulation of Cass as a kind of slave, Mason refuses to let him have a drug that Michele needs, until "you come to your senses." On the fatal night of the Hollywood party, Mason rapes Francesca; the hotel proprietor tells Cass later that she has been found beaten to death, and Cass chases Mason up a cliff to fling him off. Luigi, aware of Cass's long, self-pitying bout with alcohol and guilt, decides not to prosecute, in order to end once and for all his self-indulgent wallowing. Saverio, the village idiot, who did kill Francesca, will be taken care of. Michele dies, but Cass feels reborn: "Ripeness is all." And Luciano di Leito, a young man whom Leverett had run down on the road to Sambuco, suddenly fully recovers in the hospital, a phoenix risen from his own ashes: "He will live to bury us all" (*SHF,* 513).

Such is the skeletal outline of Styron's third novel in its intricate, technicolor recounting of Leverett's personal doubts, Kinsolving's spiritual agonies, Flagg's ritualistic death, and Luigi's remarkable interference with the law to set things right. But of course Styron is grappling with larger issues and more enigmatic concerns.

Visceral Visions

Foremost among these is the vision of America and the decline of the West, a scathing follow-up to Styron's gentler attack on the materialism of the fifties in *Lie Down in Darkness.* Alfred Leverett, Peter's father and an irascible prophet-spokesman of doom and loss, attacks America's false gods, its "moral and spiritual anarchy," the rootless ennui and waste of the Eisenhower years. Styron upbraids the Reverend Dr. Irvin Franklin Bell (read Norman Vincent Peale) for his "simple moral equation of wealth and virtue, virtue and wealth, as easy to abide by as to understand" (*SHF,* 103). Of course the Hollywood folk, neck-deep in their commercial carnival, have "no kinship with tragedy" (*SHF,* 237), and the American spirit in general, mired in materialism and consumerism, festers in a "land where the soul gets poisoned out of pure ugliness" (*SHF,* 289).

As a result of American wealth, Americans "have to drink because drinking drowns their guilt over having more money than anybody in the world" (*SHF,* 353). And is it no wonder that the suffering artist Cass Kinsolving has to flee that "soft-headed, baby-faced, predigested, cellophane wrapped, doomed, beauty-hating land" (*SHF,* 371)?

As usual, Styron finds a psychological theory to prop up his outrage. Such a place, "the bleeding shallow and insincere epitome of a bleeding neo-yahoo snakepit of a fifth-rate juvenile culture that only a moron could live in" (*SHF,* 403), exercising "its childish glorification of scoundrels and nitwits and movie trash, and its devotion to political cretins" (*SHF,* 404), is, as Alfred Leverett brands it, "a nation of children" (*SHF,* 15). "*Children! My Christ! All of us!*" (*SHF,* 473) bewails Cass, and the only way to break out of this cocoon is to "bring back tragedy to the land of the Pepsi-Cola and the

peanut brittle and the Modess Because" (*SHF,* 121). Alfred Leverett con-
curs: "What this great land of ours needs is something to happen to it.
Something ferocious and tragic, like what happened to Jericho or the cities
of the plain—something terrible I mean . . . so that when the people have
been through hellfire and the crucible, and have suffered agony enough and
grief, they'll be men again" (*SHF,* 15).

In order to achieve genuine tragedy, to be "men again," of course, individuals must be exorcised in some way, scoured and cleansed and set afire.
Unfortunately, in *Set This House on Fire* the oedipal morass remains intact.
Characters may cleave and kick, submit and strut, but they essentially remain the same, self-enclosed and comfortable in a large American playpen
that puts up with their antics. Their suffering remains comfortably contained within recognizable boundaries, the ennui of the well-off, safe in
their cradle of the world. We get melodrama, not tragedy, despite the
conflagration.

The oedipal scheme of things—more or less responsible fathers and
mothers, more or less guilty but paralyzed children—webs and cocoons the
novel and deprives the main characters of genuine breakthroughs, as it did
with Milton and Peyton Loftis, Tom Culver and Al Mannix. "Wendy-dear"
spoils Mason entirely: "Oh, you are the *bright* star in Wendy's crown!"
(*SHF,* 88). Wendy refers to her own father as Daddy Bob. Peter and Cass
are drawn irrevocably to Mason like childlike moths to a powerfully patriarchal flame. Celia, Mason's wife, flatters him as much as Wendy did, and
Cass, the orphan, frantically scrawls on a sketch pad, *"Children cleave to your
sire and repose from this late roaming so Forlorn so grievous!"* (*SHF,* 208).
Styron draws direct parallels between Cass and Oedipus at Colonus, and
Cass seems more drawn to the "wisdom" of grief and doom than to any notion of responsibility and tragic grandeur.

Yet in the novel Styron conjures up very visceral scenes of the horror of
real suffering, the most famous revealing the women's carrying faggots,
bent and burdened like three fates of some ancient myth of irremediable
suffering, and the dog who will not die. The women reveal only soulless
physical misery. The local doctor tries to bludgeon to death a dog that has
been run over in the road, but it continues to live, "still mouthing its silent,
stunned agony." To Cass "all seemed inextricably and mysteriously connected, and monstrously, intoleraby so" (*SHF,* 351), and in his later nightmare about the incident, the dog and peasant women become one.

Styron fills his text with images of "awful grief" and "living lamentation."
Through no one's fault, everyone is made to suffer, including Michele's wife
and Michele himself. Peter Leverett suffers nightmares filled with "cata-

clysm and upheaval . . . remote screams and yells, and wails of terror, and the anguish of the flayed and the crucified" (*SHF,* 222). In such a world, Luigi declares, "We are serving our sentences in solitary confinement . . . [left] alone with the knowledge of insufferable loss. . . . That is our condition. . . . This existence itself is an imprisonment" (*SHF,* 506, 507).

Manichaean Mysteries

From these scenes and images of suffering emerges the Manichaean vision of the novel. Asceticism or libertinism seem to be the only legitimate choices in such a place, since any hope for a Christian redemption appears impossible. No divine power can rescue anyone from it.

Styron builds on these Manichaean notions. To Michele and Luigi, God is simply evil himself. Both Peter and Luigi think that if there had been any good God, he has long since deserted his post. Cass pictures a vengeful Jehovah, as the Manichaeans pictured the Old Testament God, and views him as existing to torment mankind, to annihilate it. Our solitary confinement to a place of dying, suffering dogs unable to die confirms as much, since suffering comes without release. And if there is a God, thinks Cass, he must be far weaker than the forces of evil that seem to have taken over from him. In seeing himself as a man "who had dreamed wild Manichaean dreams," Cass reports that those dreams "told him that God was not even a lie, but worse, that He was weaker even than the evil He created and allowed to reside in the soul of man" (*SHF,* 282). Out of such Manichaean dreams can come only knowledge of grief and doom, with never a vision "over the plains of the land's swelling bosom" as in Sophocles' "Oedipus at Colonus" (*SHF,* 395). Sophocles leaves Cass "bewildered and unnerved . . . and made moist the palms of his hands" (*SHF,* 305).

And yet the Manichaean notion of evil must vie querulously with others in *Set This House on Fire,* none of them strong enough to seize the book's rhetorical sweep and shake it up into a coherent whole. The matter may be more a case of Styron's materials getting away from him—Manichaean here, Christian-humanist there, existential-romantic somewhere else—than the dubious necessity of making every scene hew some preset metaphysical line. Evil, strongly explored earlier, still remains in Styron's grasp uncertain, as Cass reveals:

This business about evil—what it is, where it is, whether it's a reality, or just a figment of the mind. Whether it's a sickness like cancer, something that can be cut out and destroyed . . . nothing much more than a temporary resident in the brain . . . or whether it's something you can't cure at all, but have to stomp on. . . . And both of these theories are as evil as the evil they are intended to destroy and cure. At least that's what I've come to believe. Yet for the life of me I don't know of any nice golden mean between the two. (*SHF*, 130–131)

Anthony Winner, in discussing how we should understand and/or judge Mason, reveals the same dilemma in the novel: if evil is an irrational guilt within Mason, then adjustment psychology can cure him. But if evil resides in man's inhumanity to man or in some other, larger realm, then a tragic humanism presides over the novel as a whole (Winner, 110–34). Styron finds it difficult to decide, and the Manichaean suffering along with the oedipal breast-beating only muddies the issue.

Perhaps Norman Kelvin provides one of the clearest answers, discovering in Styron's novels "a haphazard design in which evil is set forth in an unstable pattern, one that ultimately falls into disarray. To write about evil, to hold it in sustained focus in a novel, one must be free of sentimentality in matters relating to it. . . . The form that sentimentality takes in his work is an analytic view of the spectrum of pain. All manifestations and experiences of pain are as a result seen as equal, and whatever depth there is beneath any one of them is never fully explored" (Kelvin, 209).

As if to bridge these separate and often-conflicting notions of evil, Styron sets up a series of dualisms, of unresolvable opposites and lacerating paradoxes, throughout the text. His elaborate construction of confrontations, collisions, and encounters reflects the stuff of the American romance, with its almost allegorical intensity. Thus Mason Flagg is both "daylight squire and nighttime nihilist" (*SHF*, 161), both prudish and priapic. Celia, his wife, becomes for Peter "a large nocturnal blur," as Carole, his mistress, resembles "light, a daytime creature" (*SHF*, 159). Luigi views eternity as a dark whiteness and is both a fascist policeman and "existential" humanist. Vernelle Satterfield uneasily combines harlot and vestal virgin as a lascivious Jehovah's Witness, so much so that it causes Cass to suffer premature ejaculation. Francesca becomes both angelic peasant and seductive temptress. And, of course, Cass is viewed as a battlefield of warring impulses between the light and the dark, love and hate, springtime celebrations and suicidal yearnings. He is both a slave to Mason and a savior to Michele.

Nowhere does Styron set up his bifurcated vision better than in his representation of Italy as a "bucolic glade [echoing with] muffled sounds of toil and tribulation that were worse than grief" (*SHF*, 348). The country seduces with its colors of rust and gold; Rome glows; Sambuco can be the-atrical, stunning, and hypnotic. The Vale of Tremonti approaches Arcadia in its beauty. And yet the Italians are viewed as thieves and gangsters, cor-rupt and poor wretches, creatures mired in their suffering beings: "He [Luigi, the policeman] knew that in this country there was little chance of 'becoming'; you were what you were, and that was that" (*SHF,* 476–77). Perhaps as Anthony Winner suggests, Styron has approached Italy as many American writers, including Hawthorne, have, as "a poisoned gar-den, a kind of anti-Eden [that] inspired a consideration of the dilemmas of innocence and evil" (Winner, 113). One might extend the analogies a bit to suggest that evil in the novel may be more Italian than American, perhaps another more uncertain ambiguity that leaves the "nation of chil-dren" intact and safe from Manichaean dreams. But these ambiguities do seem to leave Styron, as Frederick Karl wrote about John Cheever, "driven ever deeper into paradoxes, unable to see any way out" (Karl, 29).

Critics like David Galloway describe Cass Kinsolving as a kind of tragic hero in the guise of a modernized version of possible Christian redemption. And Jonathan Baumbach seems to have struggled with a similar conclusion. The pattern does exist: Cass's dark night of the soul, his resurrection at the hands of Luigi, the final declaration that "Ripeness is all," and Cass's choos-ing being over nothingness "simply to choose being."

Yet such redemption feels forced and false, like the happy ending of Hawthorne's *The House of the Seven Gables.* In that romance the eloquently conjured up gloom and decay of the old Pyncheon house are suddenly tran-scended by the marriage of Holgrave to Phoebe, thus resolving the so-far-fatal feud between Maules and Pyncheons, and by the exorcism-death of Judge Pyncheon, the powerful old colonel restored in all his hypocritical manner. But Holgrave and Phoebe are mere cardboard characters in com-parison with the decayed and decaying Hepzibah and Clifford, and Hawthorne's gloating over the judge's corpse verges on the overwrought and grotesque. The same may be said of Cass's choosing being "simply to choose being," when in fact, as we shall see, being in *Set This House on Fire* can itself be the very evil shores upon which Cass has been foundering for more than five hundred pages.

In pursuing the center of this sprawling novel, it might be appropriate at this point to consider its form in more detail, so as to be able to grasp the general focus more closely and clearly. And certainly the heavy-breathing, Faulknerian rhetoric, redolent with its "foretaste of doom" and "awful sense of predestination," raises questions similar to those concerning its use in *Lie Down in Darkness.*

Beyond or within the Manichaean and humanist-Christian strains in the novel lies the hypnagogic state. Here lies "that strange moment sometimes just before you fall asleep, which is so inexplicable and indescribable and mysterious, when you're in a state that is neither sleeping nor waking but something miraculously inbetween . . . and all sorts of random memories come flooding back with this really heart-stopping and heart-rending immediacy" (*SHF,* 272). Such a state often takes precedence over other thematic concerns, and so full of these states is *Set This House on Fire* that they almost re-create Poe's self-reflexive world of terror—were it not, from my point of view, for the intrusive psychological, Manichaean, and would-be Christian explanations.

Peter Leverett consistently dreams of a prowler in "that dream of betrayal . . . of the murderous friend who came tapping at my window" (*SHF,* 126), a friend who turns out to be more fiendlike than anything else. Cass is driven to Sambuco by nightmares and hallucinations, from the "bone-breaking moment of loveliness" in all its "selflessness" and "moment of rapture" in Paris (*SHF,* 262, 273)—later described by Cass as a "sick drunken daydream" (*SHF,* 276), more fraud than mystical vision—to dreams of waterspouts, volcanoes, and storms. From these wild visions springs not only a kind of "hallucinated rhythmical schedule" (*SHF,* 429) that Cass can almost identify but also further visions of spiders on Vesuvius and the Manichaean revelations of God's weakness in the face of evil.

And yet the upshot blurs. It's as if Styron doesn't know exactly what to do with these powerful phenomena. Either they add up to nothing but a kind of undercurrent of terror and spiritual disintegration, or to interpret them too specifically adds up to too much of a blueprint for hatred and revenge. In attempting to articulate his nightmares, Cass strikes us as the author's attempting to achieve the same goal: "Passionately he tried to make the dream give up its meaning; each detail was as clear in his mind as something which happened only yesterday, yet when he tried to put them all together he ended up with black ambiguous chaos. Perhaps, he thought, it was a species of madness" (*SHF,* 320).

And here in microcosm may be the novel's failure: the inability to yoke together into some coherent pattern (a) explanations that are too clear and that undermine ambiguities in the text, such as the oedipal tensions and the Manichaean mysteries, and (b) explanations that aren't clear enough. The material, for whatever reasons, has not been digested sufficiently by the novelist, leaving, as David Stevenson has suggested, "un-novelized materials

. . . individual scenes, the individual characterizations [of which] accumulate but . . . remain inert" (Stevenson, 269).

The Corrosion of Nostalgia

Nostalgic dreams and the process of enchantment oppose the Gothic world of nightmare. And as Jan B. Gordon suggests in relation to much of Styron's fiction, "It is when history itself is called into question that memory is replaced by nostalgia" (Gordon, 105). In effect, "an aestheticization" of real events occurs, and nostalgia replaces true vision. These vast unanchored feelings, linked to childhood landscapes and southern memories, encompass the characters as pervasively as does the "doom" that threatens at any moment to capsize them. A Fitzgeraldian "sad nostalgic glamour" clings to everything like cigarette smoke to curtains the morning after a cocktail party.

Peter Leverett admits it openly: "Incorrigible to the end, I allowed nostalgia and sentimentality to win out. . . . All my life I've been addicted, in such situations, to weird self-implication" (*SHF,* 180). As classical music to Cass becomes "a form of corruption" that can act "to dope the spirit" (*SHF,* 261), and as Mozart's *Don Giovanni* in its tale of seduction can seduce with its "upsurge of sound" (*SHF,* 123), so Mason Flagg can dope and seduce both Peter and Cass "in one long fluid hot surge of remembrance and desire" (*SHF,* 420). Flagg embodies that public display of desire's limitlessness in many ways, and this fact is both his problem and Peter's and Cass's. It's as if tenderness has been separated from terror, nostalgic haze from volcanic fire, and in that sentimental breach, both tenderness and terror have equally corrupted Styron's vision.

Necessarily, nostalgia conjures up the southern strain in both Peter's and Cass's backgrounds. Peter at the beginning of the novel remembers old Port Warwick, and in his reverie it is so much more pleasant than the "pillaged town" of the present. He clings to those memories as, "in times of stress and threat, . . . people tend to hold on to the past" (*SHF,* 19). And his memory of a black man's having rescued him as a child from a tidal creek produces in him "a pure and wordless overflowing of the heart [with] a new and fathomable beauty" (*SHF,* 18). Is it any wonder why Peter could eventually be "bewitched" by the likes of Mason Flagg, given his easy surrender to such enchanted longings?

When Peter and Cass discuss the past and Sambuco, they do so in a skiff on the Ashley River. In effect they occupy the same landscape, rife with nostalgia that has followed them to Europe and back. They have never really

left it but remain "half-hypnotised by the heat and stillness and the glim-
mering noons" (*SHF,* 54), just as in Sambuco they were easily hypnotized by
the sea at night. Such reveries engulf Cass frequently with "a hundred gentle
memories, purely summer, purely southern, which swarmed instantly
through his mind, though one huge memory encompassed all" (*SHF,* 378).
It's as if Cass has moved from innocent childhood through nostalgic memories of the landscape of that childhood into his "dark night of the soul" and
safely back into the present nostalgic haze of memories recollected on the
Ashley River in the skiff with Peter. Nightmare may have disrupted nostalgia, but not for long. The self remains cocooned, no matter what happens,
in that southern miasma of memory and leaves it as encapsulated at the
novel's end as it was at the beginning.

We return to notions of the encapsulated self, for various reasons the
heart of Styron's vision once again in his third novel. What Cass hopes to do
with his hallucinations and dreams is to figure them out somehow, to strip
them naked and get to some essential revelation: "these various horrors and
sweats you have when you're asleep add up to something, even if these horrors are masked and these sweats are symbols. What you've got to do is get
behind the mask and the symbol" (*SHF,* 375). Surely this effort is a noble
one, a spiritual quest that motivates the greatest of American literature,
from Whitman's "Song of Myself" and Melville's *Moby-Dick* to John
Cheever's *Bullet Park* and Joan Didion's *Democracy.* But Cass's unmasking
reveals a different source of vision: "whosoever it is that rises in a dream with
a look on his face of eternal damnation is just ones own self, wearing a
mask, and thats the fact of the matter" (*SHF,* 371).

Cass recognizes that "to triumph over self is to triumph over Death. It is
to triumph over that beast which one's self interposes between one's soul
and one's God" (*SHF,* 260). But the triumph ultimately seems to include
the shock of recognition that the self is forever imprisoned within a hall of
mirrors in which the unmasked intruder is just the self again. Styron's vision
has revealed the self-reflexive, self-enclosed territory of Poe's "The Fall of
the House of Usher," in which every sentient thing in the universe is a projection of the self and vice versa, but Styron insists on evading that premise.
The only conclusion to such a vision is annihilation, the house set afire and
utterly destroyed, but Styron refuses to follow along the very path he himself has conjured up.

By contrast we can look at similar conditions in *Moby-Dick,* and doing so
is not unfair, since *Set This House on Fire* has much in common with the
metaphysics of that novel dedicated to the devil's deeds. Ahab, set afire by
his revenge against the white whale and the universe at large, a revenge

raised to a metaphysical and Manichaean yearning in Melville's hands, wished to strike through the pasteboard masks, all visible objects by which he felt surrounded and threatened, in order to get at the agent or principal behind them. In action itself Ahab could feel the presence of that "still reasoning thing" behind the visible objects of the universe, aware that either that presence held "inscrutable malice" toward him, as he held toward it, or that there was "naught behind," leaving the world he'd created as empty and bereft of meaning as his swollen ego could have made it. Ahab wanted to confront that "thing," to destroy language and all visible objects in the moment of action, in order to confront it—or himself—once and for all. The price of such a Faustian lust, of wanting to look directly upon the face of God or darkness, was of course Ahab's self-destruction, his death at the hands of himself or that "it" which had been unmasked. Isis unveiled is Isis dead, someone once wrote, and the same is true of Ahab's vision and his gnostic bargain.

Cass unmasks only "ones own self . . . and thats the fact of the matter." His revelation seems to incarnate only what he's already experienced, that he's locked within his own guilts and harangues to such a degree that there is "naught behind." Encapsulated in his prison of self, whether it be Manichaean, oedipal, or some crass form of American materialist consumption, that fact remains unshaken. And whatever happens to him seems to reveal that that encapsulation remains in place. There is no way out—except for Luigi's disruption of things in an act of charity that seems almost the sending of the author's deus ex machina to the rescue.

Leverett, Flagg, and Kinsolving

The three major male characters in the novel embody different facets of this essentially American—or Styronic?—encapsulated self. Styron rings changes upon them, but each repeats the same pattern, locked in his world of nightmare, nostalgic enchantment, and oedipal dependency. Peter Leverett is a more amoral Nick Carraway, a Peter Rabbit attracted to stranger gardens. In his lawyer-like, establishment manner, he seeks answers to the strange goings-on at Sambuco and is different from Cass only in that his moods are more restrained and self-controlled. He is eminently corruptible by the corrupted Mason, easily bewitched by money, the movies, and free sex, and perfectly plays his sycophantic role. He experiences the smoldering "sharp blade of nostalgia" and confused emotions that in Mason and Cass will appear as conflagrations, and cannot shake his fascination for Mason Flagg. He is convinced that Flagg "was more imaginative, more intelligent than I, and at the same time more corrupt (more corrupt, that is, than I could allow myself to be, as much as I tried) . . . he yet permitted me, in the ease of my humdrum and shallow rectitude, to feel luckier than Mason—duller but luckier, and sometimes superior" (*SHF,* 138).

Mason Flagg embodies such corruptions and corrupt enchantments and plays them for all they're worth, emboldened by his garish personality, his ability to manipulate people—who yet let him manipulate them all too easily—and his two million dollars. He's an exhibitionist, a liar, a braggart, a procurer, and an emotional leech, and covers his tracks with apocalyptic speeches about sex's being the last frontier, art's being dead, and Dionysius's being the God to save us all: "He wanted all the arts to embrace complete, explicit sexual expression. . . . He said that pornography was a liberating force, *epater le bourgeois*" (*SHF,* 450). His palaver rings hollow with "Priapean rites . . . phallic thrust . . . the penultimate orgasm" (*SHF,* 433). Only to some strangely repressed personality, already eager to be seduced and corrupted by neo-Lawrentian nonsense, can such a figure cut his kind of wide and glamorous swath.

In the end Flagg's flagging self-gratification can reveal only impotence. His collection of erotica, calculated to arouse, can only numb. His often expressed fear of women can only intimate darkly at certain repressed homosexual longings. And his sexual speeches suggest only "an empty ritualistic coupling with a machine, self-obsessed, craven, autoerotic, devoid of pleasure much less joy" (*SHF,* 419). Flagg seems a "man who had sex in the head like a tumor. . . . There's not much difference between this type and a bleeding little prude, really; both of them basically think of a good screw as something as cataclysmic as Judgment Day" (*SHF,* 449).

And yet Mason Flagg is set up as the elusive golden boy, the American dream that no one can refuse: "He was like a gorgeous silver fish in a still pond: make a grab for him, and he has slithered away. . . . He was like mercury. Smoke. Wind . . . a creature so strange, so *new*. . . . For him there was no history, or, if there was, it began on the day he was born. Before that there was nothing" (*SHF,* 454). Flagg resembles the self-creation of Gatsby; Cass and Peter need him to fulfill all the corrupting dreams within them.

Flagg's masturbatory self-indulgence is paraded like the American dream. Perhaps he really burst from the repressed and repressive fifties or the "Old South" in its death throes, not yet linked to the specific political agenda of the sixties. In any case, before Cass pushes him over the cliff, in his bedroom he screams, " 'WAH!' The sound echoed out of all childhood, a fearful, exacerbated, stricken wail—the cry of a four-year-old, terrified by dragons, thunder, or the dark" (*SHF,* 469).

Cass Kinsolving as a character has been described by critics as everything from Whitmanic to Kierkegaardian. Yet he never really escapes from the "puddle of self" that everywhere threatens to drown him. His release comes more as a result of Luigi's intervention than from his own shock of recognition. For pages and pages Cass discovers depths in himself he must wade through, filled with images of a self-sickness, self-flagellation, and self-hatred, vying to discover the final primal scream that will plummet him into self-destruction or self-recognition. Luigi acknowledges that such self-indulgence is a moral sin, that Cass sins in his omnivorous notions of guilt.

And the guilt that Cass embodies overwhelms the text. He feels guilty because he is an orphan, because he has had no formal schooling, and because he has suffered the horrors of the war in the Pacific and had to consult a psychiatrist afterward. His wife's Catholicism—his father was a Methodist minister—his artistic nature, and sex with Vernelle Satterfield produce more guilt. Guilt becomes an Anglo-Saxon legacy, the plain terror of consciousness itself, and the alcoholism of his unaccomplished days. Being American he feels guilty because of American wealth; being white he feels guilty for the black slaves brought to his native land in 1619 and for his burning down a black cabin in his youth. No wonder Luigi's explanation rings true: "You sin in your guilt! . . . You are a damnable romantic from the north, the very worst kind. In jail you would wallow in your guilt. . . . This sinful guilt . . . has made you a drunkard, and caused you to wallow in your self-pity, and made you fail in your art" (*SHF,* 499, 507–8). The failure of Cass's art reflects as well the failure of Styron's.

In the end, only death seems capable of conquering such antics, and only Mason Flagg is relieved. Cass Kinsolving escapes intact, returning to the Ashley River to impregnate the undemanding Poppy once again and to consider his seizures in Sambuco with his friend Peter Leverett. Hence he chooses being over nothingness. But the book suggests that being provides only endless guilt and irremediable suffering, one more bout with solitary confinement in a world as imprisoning as one's self. To choose such being is to choose only the relishing of such things, the impotence, however momentarily calmed, of an encapsulated self cocooned once again, if at the end in a nostalgic, exhausted haze. Being and nothingness serve as one more tag line amid the abstract detritus of Manichaean mysteries, Christian-humanist redemptions, and existential-romantic explanations.

At the end of *Set This House on Fire* the wounded Lieto, who has been languishing in a coma in a hospital since Peter ran him down on the way to

Sambuco, rises like the phoenix from his own ashes: "He will live to bury us all." But such a rising seems as chancy and accidental as everything else that has preceded it. It's a false finale, as if the author is clutching at optimistic straws in an attempt to rise out of his guilt-ridden, self-encapsulating vision.

The Result of the Fire

Critics have taken the novel justly to task. Richard Gray describes the book as "sheer bombast: Styron's attempt to make up in sheer verbal energy for what he clearly lacks in terms of substance, genuine conviction. . . . [It is] a cry for emancipation that, like Milton Loftis', remains more or less trapped in the vocabulary and values of the very systems it wishes to defeat" (R. Gray, 299). Abraham Rothberg would agree: "All too often, Styron is overwhelmed by things, by words, in that old Whitmanesque tradition . . . in which instead of artistic selection, there is enumerating, inventorying, cataloging."[3] And perhaps in this instance Norman Kelvin best sums up Styron's accomplishment at this time: "It is a curious fact that Styron's novels elude the attempt to see them whole in the mind's eye. Nor do they create the impact of calculated discontinuity that would mark the intention behind them as modernist" (Kelvin, 209). The phoenix rising from its ashes reveals an image of continuity and completion that *Set This House on Fire* has not earned.

And yet the sheer energy and scope of the novel attest to its power. It makes other novels published in 1960, such as John Updike's *Rabbit, Run* (however more successful as a novel), seem spare and juiceless. Though the intended meaning of some kind of exorcism and redemption is betrayed by the very structure in which that experience is portrayed, *Set This House on Fire* taps into that American romantic tradition of cultural allegory and Gothic confrontation which has powered such works as *The Scarlet Letter, Moby-Dick, Absalom, Absalom!* and John Gardner's *The Sunlight Dialogues.* In its intensity but not in its form, in its desire but not in the fulfillment of that aim, in its explosive rage but not in the worked-out completion of that rage, the novel may reveal its most American characteristics. It may signify ultimately the dead end of a fiftie's vision and Styron's own, the self-destruction of the architecture and themes of *Lie Down in Darkness* and *The Long March.*

The problem after *Set This House on Fire* remains essentially the same as after the first two novels: where to now? And the answer would come with Styron's never-forgotten, long-smoldering fascination with Nat Turner's rebellion and with his own southern roots.

Chapter Six

The Confessions of Nat Turner:
A Slave to History

If one of the main problems in Styron's fiction so far had been the tendency to isolate the individual self from anything larger and to isolate it in a cocoon of self-flagellation and despair linked uncertainly to American consumerism and its childish culture, then one way out would be to link that self more firmly to something larger, to implicate it in history and to anchor it in a historical context that at the same time could help define that individual temperament and character. What Styron seems to have needed is a historical truth he could not tamper with, the kind of truth that Truman Capote came up against in *In Cold Blood* or that Norman Mailer did in *The Armies of the Night*: "I like the feeling that something is happening beyond and about me and I can do nothing about it," Capote once explained. "I like having the truth be the truth so I can't change it" (Clarke, 317). What better antidote than this to Styron's dilemma of the encapsulated and isolated self?

From his childhood Styron had been aware of Nat Turner's rebellion in 1831. It had happened close to where he grew up. He had continuously thought about it. And here he was confronted with a real rebellion, "blessed" with the confrontational realities of black and white, slave and master, prisoner and jailer. What better way to counteract the seductive mire of nostalgia and guilt in himself, or in his previous characters and the prose that had created them, than to grapple with history itself? Couldn't he use historical fact to buttress his fascination with solitary individuals, to reconstitute them in an actual historical context that would necessarily transcend his solipsistic sense of guilt and paralysis? History could provide that self with an actual tragic experience, to involve it in social complexities and cultural contexts that had actually existed.

Styron had always relied on what Frank Lentricchia has described as the modernist myth, that neo-orthodox vision of pitting the self against the unmediated chaos of history and life itself, what Robert Frost once described a poem as being: "a momentary stay against confusion." For Lentricchia, "the idea of reality as a chaos is, since Nietzsche, a casual assumption, one of modernism's characterizing shibboleths. . . . [The modernist writer] has a need . . . to project a myth of unbearable chaos as the enabling condition of the modern sensibility . . . by constructing a starkly agonistic image of the self's confrontation with its world."[1]

Lentricchia's argument does characterize much of the central focus of Styron's fiction, a focus to which Styron has often succumbed and from which history might be able to extricate him. Self-consciousness is not enough, for it has led in Styron's fiction to what Lentricchia defines as "the modernist intellectual's rationalization of his alienation and impotence" (Lentricchia, 57), that attempt to withdraw from all action in the recognition that nothing will succeed, which hovers around Styron's characters such as Cass Kinsolving, Milton Loftis, and Tom Culver. From such a perspective a historical context could free that self from belaboring its self-consciousness to the point of paralysis.

History and Fiction: A Clash of Constructions

Grappling with history raises several questions about the relationship between history and fiction, questions that surfaced particularly at the time Styron was writing *The Confessions of Nat Turner* but that have always been extant. "History, not literary aesthetic, dictates sensibility and belief in twentieth-century literature," declared George A. Panichas in his book on politics and literature, since ours is a decidedly historical age, one in which "the traditional role of the writer as storyteller has merged with what can be termed the prophetic role, whereby the writer in his art combines craft with moral and ultimately apocalyptic meaning—becoming a 'spokesman of tragic times' of whom much is expected."[2]

In 1965 Truman Capote's *In Cold Blood* was published, a literary phenomenon that Capote described as a nonfiction novel. "Journalism," he said, "always moves along on a horizontal plane, telling a story, while fiction—good fiction—moves vertically, taking you deeper and deeper into character and events." As Gerald Clarke makes clear, Capote "was fenced in by the barbed wire of fact," but within those boundaries he enjoyed the "freedom to juxtapose events for dramatic effect, to re-create long conversations," and in short to inject all his fictional images, themes, and motifs that he had always relied on (Clarke, 357).

In 1967 Norman Mailer's *The Armies of the Night* appeared, and Mailer too took on the differences and similarities between history and fiction, describing his book as "History as a Novel, The Novel as History." For him history had to be "scrupulous to facts, and therefore a document," but when the writer wished to probe a more interior reality, "the novel must replace history at precisely that point where experience is sufficiently emotional, spiritual, psychical, moral, existential, or supernatural." At that point the writer "will now unashamedly enter that world of strange lights and intuitive speculation which is the novel." Though Mailer's definition of the novel fits more squarely with the American romance, still his recognition "that an explanation of the mystery of the events at the Pentagon cannot be developed by the methods of history—only by the instincts of the novelist"[3] —reflects Capote's view that it is up to the novelist to bore within and intuit the significant depths of characters and events. These kinds of techniques were employed as well by such self-declared "New Journalists" as Tom Wolfe at the time.

Styron had his own explanations of what he had tried to accomplish in *The Confessions of Nat Turner.* "A work which deals with history can at the same time be a metaphorical plan," he explained in 1968, after the ten black writers' response to his novel, "a metaphorical diagram for a writer's attitude toward human existence, which presumably is one of the writer's preoccupations anyway." Styron had already wrestled with issues of human domination and submission and with the uncertain means and ends of rebellion in many of his characters, and certainly the history of slavery and of Nat Turner's failed revolt in his native Virginia couldn't help but reflect that similar "metaphorical diagram." At the same time he opposed mere fact as the basis for a convincing fictional narrative: "A brute, an idiotic preoccupation with crude fact is death to a novel, and death to the novelist."[4]

Perhaps R. G. Collingwood's discussion of history as a reenactment comes closest to what Styron had in mind when he called his novel "less an 'historical novel' in conventional terms [by which he seems to have meant a kind of simplistic costume drama of stereotypical characters cavorting in some cardboard pageant] than a meditation on history" ("Author's Note," *CNT*). "The historian," Collingwood asserts, "must re-enact the past in his own mind," and such a process of reenactment must involve the emotional and the subjective as well as the logical and intellectual deductions of the historian. A historian can never merely believe what witnesses to history have witnessed, but must get beyond the "relics" of "written words . . . [and] discover what the person who wrote those words meant by them. This means discovering the thought . . . in the widest sense of that word . . . which he expressed by them. To discover what this thought was, the historian must think it again for himself."[5]

What this perspective suggests for our purposes is that Styron's meditation on history is both a meditation on Nat Turner's role in history and a re-creation of Nat Turner's own meditation on that role. The result can be confusing, as we shall see, since it is often difficult within the novel to distinguish between Styron's interpretation of Nat Turner's accomplishments and Nat Turner's "own" assessment of his life. But Collingwood's reenactment theory does help us examine more closely what Styron meant by "meditation" and whether or not he succeeded in fulfilling that notion.

Gray's Nat and Styron's Turner

On many points Thomas R. Gray, the original transcriber of Nat Turner's actual confession, and William Styron agree in terms of who Nat Turner was and what he did. Their disagreements suggest in many cases the novelist's need to fill in the blanks and add greater detail to his story rather than Styron's twisting facts to suit his own uncertain ends. Yet discrepancies do exist and leave some questions unanswered.

Styron quotes verbatim two large chunks of Gray's *Confessions* and in several instances repeats the biblical verses Gray's Turner quoted. The two large quotations confirm Nat Turner's awareness of his own uniqueness and sense of mission and appear at the beginning of Styron's novel. Here Nat declares that others said to him as a child, "I surely would be a prophet," and he himself grew up with a sense of "my superior judgment," deciding early on to seek "Divine inspiration" and avoid "mixing in society, wrapping myself in mystery, devoting my time to fasting and prayer" (*CNT,* 24, 26). And even though Styron emphasizes the Old Testament rage and vengeance in Turner's vision, both he and Gray report that Turner felt no sense of guilt. "Do you not find yourself mistaken now?" Gray asks him. "Was not Christ crucified?" Turner replies.[6] At the trial Gray's Turner pleads, "Not guilty," but Styron's Turner exclaims, "I don't feel anything . . . I don't feel any guilt" (*CNT,* 318–19).

Gray's portrait of Turner is stereotypically simple: he is a fanatic and a fiend. The man's "gloomy fanaticism" and "fiend-like face" reveal a mind that is "dark," "bewildered," "overwrought," "remorseless," "confounded," and "corrupted," "endeavoring to grapple with things beyond its reach." He appears as a "warped" and "perverted" individual whose obsessions overpower him, "not instigated by motives of revenge or sudden anger, but the results of long deliberation, and a settled purpose of mind." All is "the offspring of gloomy fanaticism" (Gray, 97). Jeremiah Cobb agrees, viewing him as *"borne down by this load of guilt* [as] *the original contriver of a plan* [of] *plotting in cold blood"* (Gray, 116).

And yet even Gray cannot help but acknowledge Turner's uniqueness.

He recognizes his "natural intelligence and quickness of apprehension," his ability to read and write, his "purity" in that he was never one "to swear an oath, or drink a drop of spirits." Turner is also not a coward but acted decisively when he realized "it was better to surrender, and trust to fortune for his escape." And Gray marvels at the imprisoned slave's "daring to raise his manacled hands to heaven, with a spirit soaring above the attributes of man; I looked on him and my blood curdled in my veins" (T. Gray, 113).

As a fanatic, Nat Turner fits Gray's presentation of him well. Gray goes out of his way to prove that Nat is at fault, not the institution of slavery. This is the work of a "gloomy fanatic," not the result of social oppression: "It is the first instance in our history of an open rebellion of the slaves" (T. Gray, 95), but it is the result of Nat Turner's long deliberation and obsession, rather than motivated by revenge and anger. Turner is the evil culprit; the system remains intact. And Gray buttresses his argument with examples of loyal slaves who rescued Miss Whitehead and Mrs. Baron. Society, therefore, generally continues to wear "a calm and peaceful aspect" (T. Gray, 96).

Gray, a creature of the Age of Reason, goes out of his way to point out the rational laws that uphold the community at large and the demonic blacks who tried to undo them. Citizens would be glad to know that "the policy of our laws in restraint of this class of our population . . . are strictly and rigidly enforced. Each particular community should look to its own safety, whilst the general guardians of the laws, keep a watchful eye over all." All the conspirators "were shot down in the course of a few days, or captured and brought to trial and punishment." And the good community folk can read "an awful, and it is hoped, a useful lesson as to the operations of a mind like" Nat Turner's (T. Gray, 97).

As for the slaves, they can be nothing more than "diabolical actors," a "band of savages," a "fiendish band," and "ferocious miscreants" (T. Gray, 95–97). The "true negro face, every feature of which is strongly marked," resembles "the expression of [Nat's] fiend-like face" (T. Gray, 113). The demons showed no mercy; they killed women and children as well as men. Their only restraint seemed to be "apprehension for their own personal safety . . . and it is not the least remarkable feature in this horrid transaction, that a band actuated by such hellish purposes, should have resisted so feebly, when met by the whites in arms. Desperation alone, one would think, might have led to greater efforts" (T. Gray, 96).

Gray supports his argument by using the sentimental images the Age of Reason cherished in its often-sentimental discourse: "It will be long remembered in the annals of our country, and many a mother as she presses her infant darling to her bosom, will shudder at the recollection of Nat Turner, and his band of ferocious miscreants" (T. Gray, 97). The little girl who managed to escape the massacre explained that "the Lord helped her" (T. Gray, 114). And John T. Baron's bravery "saved from the hands of these monsters, his lovely and amiable wife" (T. Gray, 115).

Yet there are cracks in the fanatic's armor that a novelist couldn't help but exploit. Jeremiah Cobb said of Turner, "your only justification is, that you were led away by fanaticism" (T. Gray, 116). If fanaticism was Turner's justification, then that suggests he may have been using it as an excuse to cover his tracks. And Gray himself admits: "He is a complete fanatic, or plays his part most admirably" (T. Gray, 113).

When it comes to the events that Gray and Styron describe, these events are remarkably similar. In the events prior to the revolt itself Styron emphasizes Turner's rage, but he also makes more out of "black power" and Turner's ability to organize his troops and his plans than Gray does. In Gray's *Confessions* Turner escapes from an overseer but returns after thirty days, convinced that the Spirit has told him to "return to the service of my earthly master. . . . And the negroes found fault, and murmured against me, saying that if they had my sense they would not serve any master in the world." At about this time Turner undergoes a vision of "white spirits and black spirits engaged in battle, and the sun was darkened" (T. Gray, 102). In Styron's text there is no mention of Turner's thirty-day escape or of the blacks' murmuring against him. And the vision is far more explicit: "and the two spirits were locked in celestial battle high above the forest. . . . Yet . . . the white angel was vanquished and his body was cast down through the outermost edges of the sky. Still I gazed upward where the black angel rode triumphant among the clouds" (*CNT,* 236). The details of the darkening sun, the roar of thunder, and the flowing blood remain the same, but Styron has sharpened the contest and given victory to the black angel.

If Gray's Turner emphasizes Christ and redemption, Styron's emphasizes war and blood more reminiscent of the Old Testament. The biblical quotations are similar, but Styron's Turner is far more vengeful and alienated in his anger.

In many ways Styron's Turner comes across as having plans better thought out in advance than Gray's Turner does. Gray makes clear that during the eclipse of the sun in February 1831, Turner decided to tell Henry, Hark, Nelson, and Sam about his plans for a revolt. Styron's Turner has already set forth his plans in detail and lined up his friends, waiting only for a moment like the eclipse to set them in motion. Gray's Turner cannot attack on 4 July as planned, because "I fell sick, and the time passed without our coming to any determination how to commence" (T. Gray, 104).

Styron's Turner cannot attack on 4 July, because "for the first time in local history" the holiday will be celebrated in the town of Jerusalem, and it would be impossible to seize the armory there with the town filled. As of Saturday, 20 August 1831, Gray's Turner and his friends were still eager "to concert a plan, as we had not yet determined on any" (*CNT,* 104–5). Then on the night of the revolt, Styron's Turner sends Henry and Will back to murder the infant in the cradle at the Joseph Travis house. Gray's Turner does no such thing, implying that Henry and Will return on their own.

In re-creating the rebellion itself, Gray's *Confession* lists the people murdered, up until the final unraveling of events. Gray's Turner describes the brutal procession from the Travises' house to Salathul Francis's, Mrs. Reese's, Mrs. Turner's at sunrise, and Mrs. Whitehead's. At the Whiteheads' Will kills Richard and his mother. Nat commits his only murder, killing Margaret Whitehead with sword blows and a fence rail. At the Porters' the family has escaped to spread the alarm of the uprising. With fifty or sixty men Turner decides to start for Jerusalem, but in a series of skirmishes the blacks retreat, after first causing the whites to flee. The attack on Jerusalem is no longer possible, and with forty men and sentinels at Major Ridley's place, another attack is launched by the whites, many blacks flee, and Turner's forces are reduced to twenty.

Turner realizes on the night of Wednesday, 24 August, that all is lost, for at the Harris farm all but two have deserted him. And even they vanish—Turner thinks they have been captured—as Turner, after trying to regroup, flees into a hiding place for six weeks. A dog discovers and steals meat from his "hole under a pile of fence rails in a field," the hole is quickly discovered by two blacks whom Turner knows "would betray me," and Benjamin Phipps captures him, "pursued almost incessantly until I was taken a fortnight afterwards" (T. Gray, 111–12).

Styron chooses to emphasize, with Thomas Gray as his mouthpiece in places, why the rebellion failed—the attack at the Ridleys when the rebellion comes apart, the battle between Will and Turner for leadership of the disintegrating rebellion, Turner's killing Margaret Whitehead, and Turner's allowing a white girl to escape from the Harris farm to spread the alarm, knowing that all has proved futile. Styron's reasons for the failure of the revolt match those which Gray's Turner gives: the drunkenness within Turner's forces, the failure of more blacks to rally to the cause—Turner's forces dwindle from sixty to forty to twenty to two—and the loyalty of some blacks to their masters. The recognition of the shattering of the mission at the Ridley farm parallels Gray's Turner's explanation of it.

Styron does characterize Will and Margaret Whitehead more than Gray has time to do, a subject we will examine, especially in terms of Whitehead, when we look more closely at the characterizations within the novel. Margaret pleads for Turner to finish her off, but Styron's Will is far more a self-righteous machine of hatred than practically anyone else in the book.

In Gray's *Confessions,* when Will joins Turner's forces, Turner describes it in rational terms: "I . . . asked Will how came he there, he answered, his life was worth no more than others, and his liberty as dear to him. I asked him if he thought to obtain it? He said he would, or lose his life. This was enough to put him in full confidence" (T. Gray, 105). The conversation sounds like the genteel discussion of two eighteenth-century gentlemen. On the other hand, Styron's Will reveals a "demented, murderous, hate-ravaged, mashed-in face" (*CNT,* 305). Styron has chosen to elevate or re-duce him to a murderous conspirator, dying to spill white blood at all costs. While this portrait of Will may be an exaggeration—and there stands a good argument: why cannot Will be more maddened by his anti-slavery notions of liberty than by his own demented and tormented soul? —Gray's *Confessions* do reveal Will as a consummate murderer. Will kills; Turner does not. Will kills Mrs. Turner, and when Turner is unable to kill Mrs. Newsome at the Turner farm, Will kills her, too. He also kills Richard Whitehead, whereas Styron has Hark and Henry, friends of Turner, dispatch the Calvinist clergyman.

Thus the scene in Styron's novel between Will, the man of action, and Turner, the man of indecision, is at the very least historically correct. Gray's Turner admits that "I never got to the houses . . . until the murders were committed, except in one case" (T. Gray, 108). He tries again and again to kill but fails. He is unable, for instance, to kill Joseph Travis: "it being dark, I could not give a death blow, the hatchet glanced from his head." Will has no problem with the dark: "he sprang from the bed and called his wife, it was his last word, Will laid him dead" (T. Gray, 105). Styron's tendency to fasten on the psychological at the expense of the historical may account for his portrait of the bloodthirsty Will, but that portrait complies with the facts as stated in Gray's *Confessions.*

One basic discrepancy remains in regard to Turner's family, and Styron's choices here do minimize the influence of Turner's black family on him and maximize the influence of the whites. According to the origi-nal *Confessions,* "my [Turner's] father and mother strengthened me in this my first impression, saying in my presence, I was intended for some great purpose" (T. Gray, 99). In Styron's novel appears only "my mother strengthened me in this my first impression . . ." (*CNT,* 99). This omis-sion is strange, since fathers play such a strong role in Styron's other fiction, and it does leave the door open to charges of racism. Styron has chosen to emphasize the whites' influences on Turner's growing up and has eliminated most of the blacks'. Styron replaces Turner's "grandmother, who was very religious, and to whom I was much attached" with "my mother, to whom I was much attached," thus truncating generational influences on Turner's childhood and eliminating the description of the grandmother as "very religious."

Gray maintains that Turner "can read and write, (it was taught him by his parents)" (T. Gray, 113), even though in an earlier instance, it is not exactly clear who taught him: "The manner in which I learned to read and write . . . [led to] the astonishment of the family, one day, when a book was shewn to me to keep me from crying [and] I began spelling the names of different objects" (T. Gray, 100). While "the family" does not specify white or black, in context it seems to suggests Turner's own black relations. This aspect Styron has neglected to pursue. Gray's Turner maintains that "I had been taught to pray [by] both white and black" (T. Gray, 101), but Styron eliminates the black influence and emphasizes instead the influence of the whites, such as that of Nat's owners at the time, Samuel and Nell Turner: "So near to the white people, I absorb their language daily . . ." Nat insists (*CNT,* 114). He adds that he has "become the beneficiary (or perhaps the victim) of my owner's zeal to tamper with a nigger's destiny" (*CNT,* 125). It is the whites who spent so much time "drilling me in the alphabet and teaching me to add and subtract and, not the least fascinating, exposing me to the serpentine mysteries of the Episcopal catechism" (*CNT,* 126).

The discrepancies between Gray's and Styron's accounts of Nat Turner's upbringing and of the influences on him are probably the most serious and do raise real questions about Styron's reasons for creating them. His white southern background may have dictated no other choice, and a certain racist specter hovers over those choices. And it is to the charges the ten black writers made against Styron's novel—at the height of the hot political climate of the midsixties—that we should now turn to examine the arguments and condemnations therein.

The Attack by Ten Black Writers

The level of invective and flammable rhetoric with which several black writers attacked *The Confessions of Nat Turner* in *Ten Black Writers Respond* (1968) has much more to do with the year in which it was published than with the nature of the attack itself. Yet a systematic review of the most substantial charges, now that the dust has settled—or has at least been shifted in the passage of twenty-odd years—is one other way of approaching and trying to assess Styron's achievement in his fourth novel.

Styron himself is the first to admit, as he did in an interview with Dick Cavett in 1979, that "all of us are bigots and racists at heart. . . . We live in a racist era." He also described Stingo in *Sophie's Choice* as "trying to exorcise his racism" (Cavett interview), a comment that reflects Styron's own processes of thought and feeling. Any discussion of this subject should make clear that the United States has enjoyed only some twenty-plus years—and these since the midsixties—without slavery or institutionalized segregation in place. The arrival on these shores of black slaves one year before the arrival of the Pilgrims puts the matter in a chilling historical perspective.

We've already discussed Styron's elimination of the influences that Turner's own black family had on his education and outlook and of Nat's elevation of Samuel Turner in that role, based on the evidence from Gray's *Confessions*. As Mike Thelwell makes clear, "The figure of Marse Samuel is familiar: a landed Virginia gentleman, for whom slavery is not a financial operation, but the exercise of a moral obligation. . . . This is the golden age of southern chivalry, and what is being reconstructed for us is the enlightened benevolence of the 'Old Dominion' version of slavery."[7] Even Thomas Gray in Styron's novel makes the case against Mississippi and Alabama but for Virginia in terms of the kinds of slavery that exist in either place. Lerone Bennett, Jr., in this regard describes Turner's mother as "an African native, who hated slavery," but he prefaces this remark by the caveat "according to tradition."[8] Tradition offers no real evidence in this case, but the entire issue does raise legitimate questions about Styron's reasons for depicting Turner's education as he does.

The whole issue about Nat Turner's having a wife seems to me a moot point, since Thomas Gray never mentions her, and the only evidence seems to be Thomas Wentworth Higginson's mention of her in his article in the *Atlantic* in 1861, thirty years after the rebellion: "we know that Nat Turner's young wife was a slave; we know that she belonged to a different master from himself; we know little more than this, but this is much."[9] Higginson never makes clear how he knows these things. Some have suggested that he found the information in a newspaper, the Richmond *Enquirer,* but the evidence seems uncertain at best.

According to Ernest Kaiser, a brief account of Turner's wife appears in Samuel Warner's *The Authentic and Impartial Narrative of the Tragical Scene of the Twenty Second of August, 1831,* but for the most part the only evidence for her existence rests with "a rich tradition"[10] and the statement Bennett makes that "Higginson's report is supported by the oral tradition" (Bennett, 11). Richard Gray may sum up the issue best when he explains, "The wife was an addition to the story made by later Northern historians (motivated, needless to say, by feelings of genuine sympathy). . . . There is nothing to prove that Turner was married, any more than there is anything to prove he was not" (R. Gray, 298).

The ten black writers did object to Styron's notion that Turner's was "the only effective, sustained revolt in the annals of American Negro slavery." Critics have cited Cato's 1739 revolt in South Carolina, Denmark Vesey's in Charleston in 1822, and Gabriel Prosser's in 1800. Thomas Gray in his *Confessions* mentions an uprising at the time in North Carolina. Some have suggested that there were seven such rebellions in Turner's lifetime: "Aptheker shows that Nat Turner's revolt was the culminating blow of a period of rising slave unrest which began about 1827 and played itself out in 1832" (Kaiser, 55). The issue here may revolve around what constitutes an "effective" and "sustained" revolt and may have more to do with myth—the power of Turner's revolt and its lasting consequences in the public mind—than with historical realities. Richard Gray concludes, "The belief that there were ever any serious revolts besides Turner's is based on evidence concocted by Herbert Aptheker [The Marxist historian]—out of memories of strikes, plots scotched in the hatching, and rumors of rebellion" (R. Gray, 298). The issue remains one for historians to explore from their various perspectives, but certainly Styron chose from his point of view the most memorable and frightening rebellion in his own native state.

It is true that Styron accepted Stanley Elkin's "Sambo" theory of slavery, which Kaiser describes in rather apocalyptic terms as the interpretation "that American slavery was so oppressive, despotic and emasculating psychologically that revolt was impossible and Negroes could only be Sambos" (Kaiser, 54). Elkin's thesis suggests that slavery as a system dehumanized people, so that it made resistance improbable. Such closed systems as slavery and concentration camps reduced the slaves and inmates to victims, in many ways dependent on the relationship with their captors. Revolt was not impossible, nor was emasculation and "Sambo-hood" the only alternative, but such systems certainly played upon human fears and weaknesses. And in his novel Styron was certainly out to expose the inhumanity of the slave system.

The truly difficult issues arise when one examines Styron's attitudes toward the black characters as individuals and toward them as a group. It is always hard to know how much and what kind of symbolic weight to impose on individual characters and incidents in a novel. Similar details can produce radically different interpretations. At the same time there are confusions between the notions of nurture and nature: are many of Styron's details meant to expose the conditions of an oppressive social and legal system? Or are they meant to suggest certain generic black traits or qualities that exist no matter what system was in place? However one feels about slavery, in Virginia in 1831 it was a historical reality supported by legislation. And the dilemma comes when something so reprehensibly and morally evil could, at one time, be defended as legally right.

There are clear-cut instances within the novel where Styron reveals how the system itself dehumanizes and influences both blacks and whites. Hark describes one condition as "black-assed . . . that certain inward sense . . . that every Negro possesses when, dating from the age of twelve or ten or even earlier, he becomes aware that he is only merchandise, goods, in the eyes of all white people devoid of character or moral sense or soul" (*CNT,* 43). Black children find themselves with nothing to do, existing "in a monotony . . . all unaware that soon they will be borne down for life with harness, chain, and traces" (*CNT,* 113). They realize early that black skin signifies no freedom; they live in fear of being sold; they recognize that in such a society to be white is to be a possessor of power and status. They must watch out for the white sport of "nigger-needling" and must listen to every white person's tone to see how they should respond in a certain instance. Their proximity to whites forces them to witness too many indignities, and they must bear the brunt of Benjamin Turner's description of them as animals, "basically as unteachable as a chicken" (*CNT,* 133). Some whites, like Samuel Turner and Jeremiah Cobb, may describe the system as a cancer and a curse, but they change nothing and would probably agree with the vision of the Episcopal clergyman, Dr. Ballard, of current conditions in 1831 as "a kind of benevolent subjection" (*CNT,* 132), the kind that Styron reveals for the most part to be a lie.

In such a system blacks are forced to assume roles to both placate and hide their real selves from their white masters. Styron describes these several disguises, the public posturing a slave must maintain to survive, "the unspeakable bootlicking Sambo, all giggles and smirks and oily, sniveling servility." They must defer, play the "obsequious coon . . . convey an impression of earnest simplicity . . . tell dumb jokes on themselves, learn to shuffle and scrape for their owners" (*CNT,* 45, 44, 191, 217). Styron makes clear that the system demands such obeisance, that these are roles played by blacks for self-preservation, and that their "most cherished possession is the drab, neutral cloak of anonymity [they] can manage to gather around [themselves]" (*CNT*, 52). Turner can see in Hark "the face of an African chieftain—soldierly, fearless, scary, and resplendent in its bold symmetry," and he mourns for the disguise Hark must wear in the presence of his white masters, that face reduced "to a kind of harmless, dull, malleable docility" (*CNT*, 45). Even Turner himself recognizes the need for role playing, deciding "upon humility, a soft voice, and houndlike obedience" (*CNT*, 218).

At one point Styron describes the infatuation Turner experiences for Miss Emmeline: "In later life, of course, I learned that such an infatuation for a beautiful white mistress on the part of a black boy was not at all uncommon" (*CNT*, 144). In this instance Turner comes upon Emmeline's having sex with her cousin Lewis and listens to the blasphemies she cries out, thereby thinking of her as an idol defiled, a saint "disrobed." His own notions of sex as violence, rape, and violation we'll examine in closer detail in the section that follows, in relation to Styron's creation of Margaret Whitehead.

With that said, there are several instances in the text where the distinction between nurture and nature is less certain and where a real confusion exists in terms of whether Styron is upbraiding the oppressions of a particular social system or revealing what he believes to be innate black traits. At the same time, Turner is aware of his own superiority in his own eyes in terms of his being able to read and write, and his epithets against his own people may be the result of this newly developed sense of pride and self-importance. Turner, for instance, as a house servant considers those who work out in the fields as unquestionably beneath him. "Though it is a painful fact," Turner states, "that most Negroes are hopelessly docile, many of them are filled with fury" (*CNT*, 46), yet the description of docility lingers uneasily in the mind. Many black boys have been "half drowned from birth in a kind of murky mindlessness"; "most Negroes become accustomed sooner or later, no matter what the occasion," to "that mood of resignation." Turner explains, "It is rare enough that I encounter a Negro with spiritual aspirations"; "Was it not fact . . . that there was something stupidly inert about these people, something abject and sluggish and emasculate" (*CNT*, 164, 172, 273, 313)

In such instances Styron walks a thin line between racist system and racial self, between the conditions of a people and certain innate traits. On these occasions black critics seem justified in pointing out the discrepancies. Why, for instance, must Turner describe the smell of black cabins as full of "the stink of sweat and grease and piss and *nigger* offal, of rancid pork and crotch and armpit and *black toil and* . . . [italics mine]" (*CNT*, 149)?

Sexuality and Margaret Whitehead

Many of the black critics take issue with Styron's handling of Turner's sexuality. Over and over again the ten black writers speak of Styron's Turner as "a kind of self-castration,"[11] a homosexual, an impotent celibate, and an emasculated male. They are infuriated at the notion that theories of sexual repression in league with the personality of a revolutionary fanatic seem to reduce a justifiable rebellion to a Freudian case history and that the sexual desire of a black man for a white woman may be more than a racist myth.

In Eldridge Cleaver's chapters from *Soul on Ice*—also published in 1968—"The Allegory of the Black Eunuchs" and "The Primeval Mitosis," Cleaver states, "I know that the white man made the black woman the symbol of slavery and the white woman the symbol of freedom. Every time I embrace a black woman I'm embracing slavery."[12] And in the latter he conjures up a kind of psychic allegory based on a class system that is itself a product of certain sexual hierarchies of power created to buttress the self-image of the class in power. The white rulers become the Omnipotent Administrators, secure in their powers of mind. They reduce the lower classes to Supermasculine Menials, creatures of body, not of mind.

The trouble occurs when the fragmented sexual image desires to be made whole, when mind seeks out body and vice versa. From such a perspective Nat Turner's lust for Margaret Whitehead becomes an understandable desire for psychic wholeness and the achievement of ultimate status in a racist society.

Whatever the psychic and sexual dimensions that Styron creates, wittingly or unwittingly, to embody the relationship he describes between Nat Turner and Margaret Whitehead, that relationship does not appear to be as momentous in terms of the novel as the ten black writers suggest. Margaret and Nat encounter each other only four times in the novel, and on that fourth occasion she pleads for him to finish his killing of her. In their first encounter she is thirteen years old, and Turner barely pays her any attention. In their second encounter, in the Whitehead library, when she reads Wordsworth to him, her apparent innocence infuriates him, and he wishes God would condemn her. In the third instance—the longest encounter Turner has ever had with a white person of either sex—she rambles on and on about "darkies" being free, full of her own Christian platitudes and insipid phrases, remarks that understandably enrage Turner and fill his mind with images of violation and rape, fraught as they are with his own notions of sex and sexual contact. It seems psychologically appropriate that forces of both desire and hatred should surge within him.

During one of his reveries in court, Turner remembers Margaret's telling him that he's one of the only people she can talk to, and he feels both sympathy and rage, confused emotions revealing the very fragmentation of self that Cleaver describes in overtly sexual-political terms. While it may be true what Frederick Karl says about her innocence—"Is there, indeed, such a thing as innocence when the very system is poisoned?" (Karl, 342)—she remains more or less an unconscious product of that system and is unaware of the effect of her sex on Turner. After all, he is merely a slave, not a man to think of in such terms. Her innocence is founded on a naive ignorance of the evil construction of the very system she's so much a part of. She cannot treat Turner as merely a friend; in such a system, fraught with its racist polarities of white master and black slave, no such social situation can really exist in and of itself. There is always a power struggle at work, and Turner recognizes that struggle in his own sexual and self-conscious confusions more than Margaret Whitehead does.

The real issue is not Turner's evaluation of Margaret Whitehead but what Styron feels about this relationship. It is one thing, after he has murdered her, to have the dazed Turner "aimlessly [circle] her body . . . the center of an orbit around whose path I must make a ceaseless pilgrimage" (*CNT,* 336–37). After all, in the novel he has spent more time alone with her than with any other white person and has undergone radical transformations in feeling, sometimes simultaneously, with her at the center of those feelings.

And yet it is quite another to suggest that she does seem to represent for Turner a kind of sentimental ideal above and beyond the black-white power plays and antagonisms. When he sees blacks standing in the hot gallery of a church, "[s]uddenly they seem to me as meaningless and as stupid as a barn full of mules, and I hate them one and all." And then he spots Margaret Whitehead singing in the crowd: "Then slowly and softly, like a gentle outrush of breath, my hatred of the Negroes diminishes, dies, replaced by a kind of wild, desperate love for them" (*CNT,* 84). Is it she or her singing that is responsible for this sudden transformation in Turner's feelings about his own people? And if so, one might ask, why does Turner need the image of a white girl to change his attitudes toward his own people from hate to love?

The final "redemption scene" in the novel—which from one point of view is no more than a masturbatory fantasy, as Turner possesses the dead white girl in his reverie, and from another suggests the possibility of love's transcending the color scheme of racial slavery—brings the issue to a head. Sex and death are once more combined. And perhaps it is the genuine *frisson* of the simultaneity of the two by which Styron in some Poesque manner is finally moved. We remember the conclusion to memories of the Turner rebellion in *This Quiet Dust:* "I thought I could hear a mad rustle of taffeta, and rushing feet, and a shrill girlish piping of terror; then that day and this day seemed to meet and melt together, becoming almost one, and for a long moment indistinguishable" (*TQD,* 30).

In any case it seems that since Margaret Whitehead is the only white Nat Turner killed, Styron was necessarily intrigued by that incident. At the same time, Turner's sexual intentions suggest rape, violation, and rage, revealing both his own self-imposed sexual restraints, as envisioned by Styron in the form of the fanatic's dedication to his mission, and the necessary violence that underlies any actual or attempted rape. Turner's lust for Margaret Whitehead is also a lashing out at that system which will not allow him to be a fully realized human being.

As Judith Ruderman has pointed out, Turner has seen sex only in terms of domination and humiliation, whether it be between his mother and the Irish overseer or Miss Emmeline and her cousin Lewis (Ruderman, 25). And his "homosexual" bout with Willis, as an unexpected prelude to his first baptism, strikes me as only an adolescent interlude, not some apocryphal moment that forever determines a person's sexual preferences. Turner's murdering Margaret Whitehead becomes an ultimate moment, wherein sexual urges, human rage, religious mission, and the desire to violate the "master race" once and for all culminate in one violent climax.

Many critics, however, have spent too much time overemphasizing a point that can never be fully fathomed and decoded. Perhaps the episodes involving Turner and Margaret Whitehead were, as many critics have suggested, a miscalculation on Styron's part, a product of his own white southern background, but it doesn't seem to cause the novel to capsize. Like many such cruxes, it is fraught with all kinds of racist, religious, and psychological dimensions, no one of which seems to overwhelm and discount another.

Language and Turner's Two Faces

Styron's Nat Turner recognizes early on that "big talk will fetch you nothing but nigger talk might work" and raises the big issue of language in the novel. John Oliver Killens describes Turner as "sometimes thinking and speaking in biblical or Victorian English and at other times lapsing into an Amos-and-Andy dialect."[13] And Thelwell derides Styron for placing "in his mouth a sterile and leaden prose that not even massive transfusions of Old

Testament rhetoric can vitalize, a strange fusion of Latinate classicism, a kind of New England Episcopalian prissiness" (Thelwell, 81).

A strong argument, however, can be made for the two modes of language Styron gives Turner to speak: one of rhetorical meditation for his inner thoughts (and this must necessarily reflect Styron's own use of language, perfectly in keeping with a novelist's art, as well as those within-the-text sources for that language which most influence Turner, such as the Episcopal catechism, the St. James Bible, and *The Life and Death of Mr. Badman*) and one of local dialect for Turner's outward expression both of the subservient role he must play as a black slave and of his role as a leader and preacher for his own people.

In effect the issue of language involves two approaches to the use of language, neither of which necessarily excludes the other. The first theory suggests that the language a character uses is first and foremost dependent on his or her role in society. Every language comes loaded with its ideological and racist subtext, so that "big talk" in the racist South is essentially a white language, and "nigger talk" remains a black dialect, the voice of the slave. Such a theory views the self as a prisoner of language, victimized by a cultural semiotics that imposes roles on the speaker without the speaker's even realizing such roles exist. The second approach connects the use of language with a measure of self-identity and self-possession. Without language, in effect there can be no self-recognition, no power to communicate. Therefore to use words is to create the self, to express a self-identity that exists not prior to language but is as completely immersed in it as fish in water. The one theory posits a predetermined social position; the second suggests the creation of a personal identity. Styron's notions of language partake of both, but they do result in some conceptual confusion.

Throughout *The Confessions of Nat Turner* Styron reveals the language discrepancies inherent in the various roles his characters are forced to play. Nat Turner himself is the most obvious example. His first thoughts about the difference between "big talk" and "nigger talk" occur when he feels himself bitterly separated from his God, an indication that his sense of language already involves his knowledge of separation and isolation. He reveals his self-proclaimed role as a prophet in language very different from that used in his role as a black slave. The language of his first sermon to his people contrasts with the language of his private visions and aspirations.

Even his confession to Thomas Gray suggests the palpable evasions of language, since he tells Gray he's had a sign from God to confess, when in fact he hopes that confession will bring him some physical relief from his chains. And Turner can easily distinguish between the manner in which

Gray talks to him and the way Gray speaks in court. One can also more readily understand the context of the sentimental drivel that Margaret Whitehead speaks with her odes and pastoral imaginings.

Styron, of course, has made "big talk" exclusively the whites' possession. Turner despises "that thick gluey cornfield accent" of field hands and the "blue-gum country-nigger talk at its thickest, nearly impenetrable, a stunted speech unbearably halting and cumbersome with a wet gulping sound of Africa in it" (*CNT,* 107, 212). His black friend "Wash has almost no words to speak at all. So near to the white people, I absorb their language daily. I am a tireless eavesdropper" (*CNT,* 114), a position that has already raised troublesome questions about the blacks' own linguistic influences on the "real" Nat Turner's upbringing. And he steals *The Life and Death of Mr. Badman* from the Turner library to "begin my laborious journey through a wild strange country where words of enraging size, black and incomprehensible, blossom like poisonous flowers" (*CNT,* 116). Such emerging powers encourage jealousy in others, such as Little Morning. And they also account for the source of Turner's rhetoric, with its biblical overtones and sonorous sweep of Styron's own.

On the other hand, wherever language comes from and however loaded it is with ideology, Styron makes plain that, as Turner suggests, to be able to spell makes him feel "wildly alive. I shiver feverishly in the glory of self" (*CNT,* 100). Jeremiah Cobb acknowledges that in learning to read and write, a slave will have "transcended his sorry state and . . . become not a thing but a *person*" (*CNT,* 54). Will's violence renders Turner speechless during the rebellion, and Thomas Gray makes it very clear, when Turner asks him to see a Bible, "that no nigger is to be allowed to read or write anyhow" (*CNT,* 89). It is the giving of the Bible by Gray to Turner at the end of the novel, on the last day of Turner's life, that initiates Turner's "self-redemption."

To Styron the writer, Nat Turner, in confessing, creates himself as a full-bodied, ambivalent, multifaceted human being. In his humanity he recognizes the alienation and isolation that have been his legacy as a black slave in a system of racial slavery. The bifurcated use of language in the novel reinforces that situation, and whatever a critic might feel about the "essence" of the rhetoric itself, it seems to embody the very process of self-division that Styron imagines to have been the product of Nat Turner's consciousness and self-awareness. Such a consciousness in no way invalidates the moral and social reasons for Turner's rebellion. If anything it humanizes the single-minded fanatic whom Thomas Gray reconstructed in his *Confessions,* as well as the single-minded revolutionary hero whom the ten black writers seem to wish "their" Nat Turner to be.

Styron's Turner: An Ambivalent Hero

"From a sixties point of view," writes Frederick Karl, "Turner should be heroic; not a man torn by human doubts but a fiery, retributive figure leading the slave revolt against inhumanity. The black critics take a social-political position on Turner, claiming him as their own" (Karl, 343). Styron himself has acknowledged as much. "They want a social myth," he replied in a 1968 interview, to a question about what black writers expected in terms of their own understanding of the historical Nat Turner. They wanted "a political tract, a call to action, and this is totally at odds with what writing a novel, a work of fiction, is all about" (Barzelay and Sussman, 101). Ernest Kaiser agreed in repeating Aptheker's sense that "reviewers of Styron's *The Confessions* have seized upon this book as pointing up the current Negro ghetto uprising as led by mad Negroes, as futile, stupid rebellions which should be put down ruthlessly" (Kaiser, 58).

The Nat Turner as presented by the ten black writers must have been "a virile, commanding, courageous figure" (Bennett, 5), as larger than life as a biblical or epic hero, convinced of his certain destiny. His motives were simple, as Killens describes them: "He was a slave, PERIOD. . . . Every slave is a potential revolutionary. . . . The master's ethics are always *enslavement;* the slave's are ever *liberation.* The liberator is the moral man" (Killens, 37). Clearly such an image appears as the flip side to Gray's gloomy fanatic. And any other image must necessarily undercut such heroic dimensions.

To the ten black writers, Styron's Nat Turner is no more than "a neurasthenic, Hamlet-like white intellectual in blackface" (Bennett, 5). He has no revolutionary desire for its own sake; he is reduced to a "religious mystic, a single-minded black believer with a powerful sense of messianic vocation"; and he is ultimately both an impotent coward and a doomed existentialist, "placed . . . totally in our own age of nothingness and fear."[14]

Styron has summarily confessed to his intentions in creating Turner's character. "I think the historical Nat Turner was an almost insanely motivated religious fanatic," he said in 1974, "and that he took literally certain messages of the Bible to be an indication that he must be a leader of an insurrection. . . . [A]s a writer I think I gave this man a dimension of rational intelligence which he most likely did not really possess, and as a result smoothed down that stark fanaticism I think was deeply buried in the man's real nature."[15] "A book like mine is showing a person too complex ever to be a proper model for revolt," Styron added. He continued, "It's showing a man who's irresolute, and who is, to be sure, a man filled with weaknesses, self-doubts. A book like *The Confessions of Nat Turner* isn't going to serve—indeed isn't meant to serve—the purposes of revolution" (Barzelay and Sussman, 102).

Turner's doubts and ambivalences, as conceived by Styron, are what drew him to the character in the first place, "the tragic notion that men in revolutions destroy so much of the thing they love; namely, they destroy their own notions of humanity by committing acts of violence against humanity. It's a paradox; it's totally unresolvable and no revolution has ever been free of it" (Forkner and Schricker, 193–194). Thus said Styron, "I wanted to risk leaping into a black man's consciousness . . . to, for the first time so far as I know, plunge a white consciousness into a black incarnation" (Barzeley and Sussman, 103, 105).

That precipitous leap produced a character caught in an anomalous role, neither merely a black slave nor obviously a free man. Styron's Nat Turner emerges from an experience rich in alienation and contradiction, a man divorced from his God, his society, and his own self, and eventually from his own sense of mission and revolt.

The notion of ambivalence helps explain the contradictions and anomalies in Turner's character, a character torn between irreconcilable voices. Vacillating between two extremes, he remains tied to a psychological framework of dualism he cannot avoid. His necessary drive to overthrow violently his white masters must insist on vanquishing whatever thoughts and feelings of common humanity he might harbor in relation to them, and his failure to achieve victory leaves him exposed, in Styron's version, to the collapse of both violence and any human feelings of remorse or sorrow.

Turner's racist society has also driven him to suppress certain aspects of himself, such as sexual desire and the desire for liberty and other basic human needs, and has forced him into a religious fanaticism so as to be able to strike out in rage and hatred at that social order of things. The forces that deny ambivalence for Styron are similar to those that seem to deny one's recognition of one's own humanity, a position that the ten black writers could see only as a luxury, like guilt and anxiety, in an evil racist world that by its very nature needed immediate destruction.

Of Turner, Styron commented that given the overriding nature of Nat's obsessions, "he must be a man of enormous frustration. Given the evidence that he didn't have a wife, this indicated some kind of singleminded, perhaps puritanical revolutionary drive which precluded the idea of fecund sexuality. After all, that kind of asceticism is a common component of the revolutionary temper" (Barzeley and Sussman, 106). Styron would add to these points his notion of Erik Erikson's *Young Man Luther,* with its "brilliant study of the development of the revolutionary impulse in a young man, and the relationship of this impulse to the father figure. Although it is best to be wary of any heavy psychological emphasis, one cannot help believing that Nat Turner's relationship with his father (or his surrogate father, his master) was tormented and complicated, like Luther's" (*TQD,* 16n).

At one point, when Nat Turner feels forced to try to read to his white audience from *The Life and Death of Mr. Badman,* he suddenly discovers that "at that moment I sensed a fatal juncture, realized with some child's wise instinct that unless instantly I asserted my small nigger self I would be forever cast back into anonymity and oblivion" (*CNT,* 124). Styron's text is riddled with such fatal junctures, those yawning gaps between reflection and action, those overwhelming situations filled with contradictions and opposing values. And Nat Turner's fate is to be stranded right in the anguished middle of them.

When we first meet Turner he is in his cell awaiting trial and aware that he has been separated from his God. That essential experience of separation determines his entire meditation on his life and revolt and establishes a motif that will resound throughout the entire novel. He feels like a fly, existing in a world of "ultimate damnation . . . eating thus, without will or choice and against all desire" (*CNT,* 21). To him "it seemed rather that my black shit-eating people were surely like flies, God's mindless outcasts, lacking even that will to destroy by their own hand their unending anguish" (*CNT,* 22). What could be taken as yet one more racist slur against his own people can also be seen as Turner's image of himself as an outcast, unable even to commit suicide and end his separation from every human and divine association.

The contradictions persist. To protect his own uniqueness, which in itself renders him an outcast, Turner must consciously wrap himself in mystery, an effort that only ensures his further isolation from everyone. While he plays the subservient "good nigger," his growing sense of his bloody mission expands, embodying the prophecies of Ezekiel, Jeremiah, and Isaiah and God's wrath. While Turner offers Hark his friendship, he also does so in order to use Hark as an "experiment," to incorporate him into his mission, failing to see that in condemning Samuel Turner's "experiment"—using Nat as a test case teaching him to read—he is essentially condemning his own technique.

Other contradictions abound. Turner's sense of self and pride develop at the same time that he recognizes he is a slave who can be bought and sold like every other slave. Samuel Turner, the benefactor, turns out to be his worst betrayer. So much for relying on the kindly master in the evil system! And interestingly enough it's when the whites feel pity that Turner is driven into his direst bouts of hatred and revenge: "beat a nigger, starve him, leave him wallowing in his own shit, and he will be yours for life. Awe him by some unforeseen hint of philanthropy, tickle him with the idea of hope, and he will want to slice your throat" (*CNT*, 56). As Turner realizes, "It was not a white person's abuse or scorn or even indifference which could ignite in me this murderous hatred but his pity, maybe even his tenderest moment of charity" (*CNT*, 216). From such contradictions emerges more clearly the rage against Margaret Whitehead.

In the third part of the novel, "Study War," the division between self and role, inner and outer language, mission and menial, and sedition and sentiment deepens and becomes incurable. The die is cast. Turner makes a conscious choice to rebel. That essential abyss into which he has fallen offers no alternatives, and neither does the racist society of which he is a victim. He is firmly aware that "I could not dislodge the sensation that I had somehow been utterly changed and now dwelt at a distance from myself, in a new world apart" (*CNT*, 246). He has accomplished the task of retreating "deeply into myself, into the vivid, swarming world of contemplation," with its "unbearable hatred for white people" (*CNT*, 231), and then "I began to suffer from that strange illusion or dislocation of the mind that from then on I could not shake loose or avoid" (*CNT*, 284). All that's needed is a crisis conversion, which finally takes place in a vision of avenging angels and in the eclipse of the sun. Now Turner is assured of his position and to his men states, "When I revealed my plans, I had insisted that they pay this deference in my presence, explaining to them patiently that I wished for no obeisance, only absolute obedience" (*CNT*, 307).

Yet contradictions and ambivalence haunt him to the end. During the revolt he cannot kill. His hatred has not prepared him for that, and it seems as though he isn't able to kill. In such a quandary Will kills. When Turner realizes the rebellion is probably lost, he allows, at the end, a white girl to escape from a farm to spread the alarm: "I suddenly felt dispirited and overcome by fatigue, and was pursued by an obscure, unshakable grief. I shivered in the knowledge of the futility of all ambition" (*CNT*, 338). Left to himself in his cell without a Bible, he feels abandoned by his God and his mission and, until the final pages of the novel, experiences only a final bitterness and withdrawal from himself, "letting the dream dwindle away from my mind, fade out—this one last time, and forever—from recollection" (*CNT,* 341).

Styron's Nat Turner emerges as both an ambivalent character and the leader of a rebellion. The character's inner turmoil does not cancel out the actual participation in and leadership of the revolt. In fact it may help to explain why Turner did not kill his victims as readily as his cohorts did. It certainly takes into consideration the many contradictions involved in the state of fanaticism, complicated by its underpinnings of religious vision, sexual tension, and hunger for violence. And it also points out the great gulf in Turner's anomalous position in a racially fractured society. Nowhere does Styron suggest, as he has in his previous fictions, that these contradictions result in a spiritual paralysis so binding that Turner is driven only by some outer forces to accomplish his ends. For once Turner's character and his actions coincide, reflecting rather than negating each other. In essence history has come to the rescue of Styron's encapsulated self and, while certain problems remain, as we shall see, the Culver-Leverett character has merged successfully with the Mannix-Kinsolving one.

The Limitations of the Black Writers' Attack

In his introduction to *Ten Black Writers Respond,* John Henrik Clarke quotes Herbert Aptheker, who defines the uses of history in his own terms: "The oppressed need it for identity and inspiration; oppressors for justification, rationalization and legitimacy."[16] While this truism is certainly provable, it does tend to reduce history to a pawn between oppressed and oppressor. Such a reduction clearly affects most of the approaches toward history in the book, since the writers want to re-create or reclaim their own image of Nat Turner as a black hero. While correct in terms of their own principles here, such a notion of the uses of history can only distort and warp other approaches. Although accurate in some instances in terms of what historical evidence is available, the black writers rely too often on "tradition" in order to shore up their image of a Turner they can defend and support.

The black writers also attack the foundations of fiction in ways they may not realize. In attacking Styron's language, use of Freudian psychology, and approach, they seem to be suggesting that no other image of Nat Turner is possible except their own. At the same time, while there is ample evidence in Styron's novel of the very racism he himself is trying to exorcise, they tend to encumber many incidents and characters with a symbolic weight these incidents and characters are unable to carry. Individuals in novels are not necessarily representatives of a group, nor do particular incidents entirely resound with the complete ideologies of the oppressor or the oppressed. Many of these questions in art remain endlessly debatable, and to close them so consistently may be to shut down art's potential for questioning all ideologies and our responses to them.

The attack of the ten black writers in 1968 is understandable, and they do make specific points that cannot and should not be set aside. But the tenor of their attack questions the uses of both history and art and reduces them to certain polemical issues; neither assumption is entirely wrong, but such authoritarian reductionism threatens other possibilities and other options.

In many ways, part of the American dream hopes to construct a world in its own image, to abolish history and view itself as the self-made creation of its own will. These ten black writers may have succumbed to such a myth, and their attack on Styron's novel upbraids it for not reproducing the kind of heroic Nat Turner they applaud. The attack is very American in its intensity and intentions, which may be one more indication of the kind of culture Styron is up against when attempting to expose the ambivalences and personal uncertainties at the dark heart of such willed visions. Turner's failure may be America's in dealing with its racist past and present and may in fact be a warning for the future against America's manner of substituting hope and myth for hard work, true commitment, and the appalling reality of its still-divided history.

Nat Turner: The Novel

What Styron has attempted to do is to reenact the growth of Nat Turner's mind and heart in a historical context. He has also structured the novel in his usual manner, creating a series of epiphanies, confrontations, and encounters that best reveal the clash between blacks and whites, individual selves and imposed roles, slaves and masters. Turner's own memory seems to circle these fateful scenes in his past in an attempt to reenact the process of his growing vision, as seen from his present state of incarceration. At the same time he vividly describes the landscape of his youth and of his life. Styron's structure mimics this meditation process, beginning as it does with "Judgment Day," with Turner confined to his cell; returning to "Old Times Past: Voices, Dreams, Recollections" to retrace Turner's development from Turner's own point of view; leading up to "Study War," when Turner determines his mission and launches his fateful rebellion; and ending with "It Is Done" by returning to the solitary Turner in his cell on the day of his execution.

Styron's withholding the rebellion to the end of the novel provides the necessary suspense in much the same way, though less successfully so, as with Flagg's murder in *Set This House on Fire* and Peyton's suicide in *Lie Down in Darkness*. The familiar techniques and structure are here, but Styron has harnessed them to a headlong historical path that streamlines his novel. As John Kenny Crane suggests, Styron has increased the tension by animating his plot in the present—the confrontation between Thomas Gray and Turner—in contrast with Turner's wrestling with his soul. This double aspect of the novel is far more dramatically successful than the relatively static presents of the hearse's journey and Cass and Peter's endless discourse in the skiff on the Ashley River in the first two novels. Finally, the very fact of the overarching shadow of Turner's imminent death provides Styron with the heady darkness he seems to need to motivate both himself and his characters.

Styron's characters for the most part emerge well rounded and whole. Hark, with a "mother's soul in the body of a bull," mourns the breakup of his family because of the slave system and becomes a killer accordingly. At one point he escapes, but not knowing anything of the surrounding geography, he merely circles the area, an image of his being still trapped in the confines of the racist society. Thomas Gray, red-faced and beefy, espouses the glories of the system, lambastes blacks with his racist epithets, and nurses his atheist pieties in contrast to Turner's seemingly fanatical belief. Yet he finally manages to smuggle a Bible to Turner on his last day, and Turner comes to understand his blind prejudice and lawyerlike logic.

Jeremiah Cobb and Samuel Turner also emerge as full-blown characters in their own right, the first a drunken widower who bemoans the curse of slavery and the eroded wasteland of his native Virginia, the second a man who appears initially like a benevolent Moses to Turner, who derides slavery as a cancer, but who in the end succumbs to financial necessity and hard times by selling Turner off like any ordinary slave. Most of the other characters—the homosexual preachers, Calvinist ranters, black slaves, "innocent" white girls—appear as sharp and singular minor portraits, products of a vicious system that shapes and directs them toward their own foreordained ends.

Certain textual problems remain. These include the quick self-redemption of Turner in the final section, Styron's own ambivalence toward his use of biblical rhetoric and religion, his use of a first-person narrator to tell the tale, and the wonderfully enigmatic dream of the white temple that haunts Turner to the end. These certainly mar the novel and raise crucial questions about it, but in the end they do not derail the careful reenactment of a doomed slave's meditating on the triumphs and failures of his life in a racist society that at the end still has the upper hand.

In "It Is Done" Nat Turner, a Bible in hand at last, is suddenly flooded by sweet memories of his past and of Margaret Whitehead. In the Bible he reads of Christ's second coming: "Surely I come quickly." The line triggers Turner's memory, and Christ's profession of love—"let us love one another: for love is of God; and everyone that loveth is born of God, and knoweth God" (*CNT,* 344)—conjures up visions of Margaret Whitehead. Overcome by that vision, Turner masturbates to it. His coming and Christ's intertwine, and Turner feels suddenly that he would have spared Margaret Whitehead if he could have, because now he understands the powers of love and sympathy that transcend all rebellion and self-isolation.

Can such a quick coming really overcome the ambivalence-ridden literary text that Styron has created up to this point? Is Styron in effect attempting to vanquish that ambivalence by suppressing it in a swift vision of reconciliation and spiritual-sexual fulfillment at the expense of the very elaborate and penetrating ambivalences he has spent time creating in his entire text? Either Turner is wildly disillusioned in his radical change to New Testament Christianity, and we are meant to take his crisis conversion as one more indication of the mad solitary, condemned to his own isolated fancies, or Styron means for us—and him—to accept what has happened as genuine. A look at the most mysterious image in the novel may make this ambiguity more understandable.

At the beginning of the novel Nat Turner sees in a dream that mysterious and windowless white sepulchre, both a temple and a sarcophagus, which "seems by its very purposelessness to be endowed with a profound mystery which to explore would yield only a profusion of darker and perhaps more troubling mysteries, as in a maze" (*CNT,* 4). This marvelous image, in its uncertain mysteries and self-enclosed remoteness, seems to embody the darker vision that lies at the heart of the novel.

Styron himself came upon it in an interesting manner:

I remember my daughter Polly telling me that she dreamed about a Masonic temple over in Woodbury. . . . Here it is, without any windows, you see, everything closed up, with the columns. And I was fascinated by her having had the dream. . . . So I put her dream and my own registry of that temple, plus something else that had haunted me. I'd seen other temples, other churches . . . all my life and had been fascinated by the mystery of the structure. . . . It's a mystery why I put it there, and Nat's a mystery, and that's a mystery within a mystery. Nat doesn't know why it's there, either, you see. (M. West, 225–26)

It reminds me of Melville's all-color, no-color "celebration" of whiteness in *Moby-Dick* and of its horrifying implications of a universe that cannot be known, of a self that cannot be fathomed, and of a text that turns back upon itself and cannot be finally unraveled.

That inscrutable white temple suggests many things. For Marc Ratner, "This temple seems to enclose the mystery of origin, the unknowable mystery of existence, the womb of timelessness . . . almost synonymous with that described . . . in Freud's *The Interpretation of Dreams* . . . the delivery of the child from the uterine waters . . . as the entry of the child into water; [from] river to ocean in this case, the ocean being freedom to expand his [soul]" (Ratner, 104). It also suggests what Evan Carton has called the "repeated conjunctions of putative opposites [as] entanglements rather than reconciliations,"[17] and what I have chosen to call Manichaean to emphasize the knotted, unresolved, continually conflicting qualities of such images. The dialectical tensions of such things suggest Turner's description, at the end of the novel, of that alabaster mausoleum of the spirit as a "white inscrutable [a favorite Melvillian word] paradigm of a mystery beyond utterance or even wonder" (*CNT,* 422).

Nat Turner, however, consciously turns away from that paradigm, "for again as always I know that to try to explore the mystery would be only to throw open portals on even deeper mysteries, on and on everlastingly, into the remotest corridors of thought and time" (*CNT,* 422). In turning away from the mystery, Turner chooses to turn toward the morning star; he avoids the former to look firmly at the latter.

It seems to me that Styron does precisely the same. He turns away from the best and most mysterious symbol in the book to the clichéd and conventional morning star in hope, perhaps, of actively controlling or willing the "resurrection" of Nat Turner from vengeance to victory. Margaret and love and God all come together as the text avoids the very image of that temple-sarcophagus-monument which threatens to annul such "resurrection." In so doing Styron clings to his thematic hopes, but in order to accomplish them, he must bury the darker mysteries his fiction has conjured up.

The ambivalences we find in Turner's character also turn up in the way Styron uses and regards his religious imagery and rhetoric. On the one hand Turner is imprisoned in the religious attitudes of his time, using religious explanations to justify his rebellion in much the same way the whites have used them to justify the status quo, as Bernard Reitz has carefully pointed out. As Styron readily concedes, "Surely Marx was right when he talked about religion as the 'opiate of the people,' because for the Southern Negro it became a *real* opiate. It *had* to be; it was the only way of life for Negroes

which made the *other* way of life, the intolerable burden of working in the
fields, bearable" (Barzelay and Sussman, 100). And religion proves to be
Turner's vehicle to transform himself from obedient slave to militant rebel.
"Possibly you can only do it if you're a religious fanatic like Nat Turner,"
Styron explained (Barzelay and Sussman, 99). Religion, therefore, becomes
the outmoded ideological manner and matter of Turner's historical period.

On the other hand Styron seems to want to convey the impression that
Turner's wrestling with his soul, his rebellion, and his failure approximate
that "dark night of the soul" which Christian saints and mystics have often
described themselves as passing through on their way to ultimate revelation.
Styron himself describes the novel as "a religious allegory; it is a story of
man's quest for faith and certitude in a pandemonious world, symbolized
by bondage, oppression. . . ." The book is a kind of symbolic representation
of the conflict between the vengeance and bloodshed of the Old Testament
and the redemption, the sense of peace and renewal, of the New Testament
(Barzelay and Sussman, 96–97).

Nat himself worries about his relationship with his God. As Styron admitted, "I wanted to get Nat after the insurrection, when he was questioning the entire relationship he had with God, with the God who had been his
guide and mentor and light throughout his life as a preacher. I wanted to
discover what was going on in his mind. . . . The relationship with God
seemed to be the central thing in my own conception of the man" (Ratner,
99). And certainly Turner is far more Christian than the likes of the Episcopalians, Methodists, and Baptists he encounters.

Richard Pearce in trying to resolve this dilemma explains that Styron is
grappling with "the conflict between Christian humanism and a world that
denies such values." In effect Styron seems to bewail the loss and denial of
humane Christian values in a world "where irrational warfare is the condition of life," and yet in evoking this very world he produces a realm "that
undermines psychological connections, temporal causation, and any kind of
certainty."[18] How can one concentrate on certain values when conjuring up a
world in which they no longer exist? Perhaps the answer lies in the ability to
see the question in terms of *both/and* rather than *either/or.* Why can't religion be both an ideological position in historical time and a transcendent
structure within which to tell the tale of that time? If religion can be used
both to justify the status quo and to awaken the faithful to battle against it,
why can't Styron use it in at least two dissimilar ways as well? Doesn't religion, then, reflect the ambivalences both in Turner's character and in
Styron's essential vision of the world?

In any case religion and religious rhetoric saturate both Nat Turner's historical epoch and Styron's imagination. Ezekiel, Jeremiah, Job, Daniel, and a host of others strike me as appropriate within the text: they provide the call to battle and the retreat from it. The Methodist Richard Whitehead and the Episcopalian Dr. Ballard use religion to uphold the status quo, in much the same manner that the Reverend Eppes uses it to arouse Pentecostal hellfire in damaged souls and as a scourge to rid himself momentarily of his own abominations. Margaret Whitehead accepts the sentimental Christian platitudes she espouses, just as Turner relies on the Old Testament to charge up his bloody mission and rouse the slaves. Baptism can be used to redeem and forgive, just as Turner's first sermon can be used to compare the ancient Jews and the black slaves in their mutual detestation of exile and bondage. And the complicated intermingling of religion and the flesh, of sermons and sex, only adds to the witches' brew of such ultimate concerns. Even Thomas Gray's attack on Christianity underlines how omnipotent it seems to be in both text and tale.

The real issue may be Styron's use of the first-person narrator. Styron has explained his decision: "For some reason, to register, to filter through the consciousness of the 'I,' the first person, is often a very powerful way of getting at immediate experience. . . . I believe the first person to be a peculiarly 1960s form of address. More and more writing is becoming first person today, because of something in the air, some psychic need for writers to address themselves in this very personal style" (Barzelay and Sussman, 103). At the same time Styron was impressed by Camus's use of the first-person narrator in *L'Etranger:* "I said to myself, 'What a nice framework this would be. I can tell the story in the first person and have it end on the day of Nat's execution.' It was the final little peg I needed to begin writing" (Ratner, 94).

As Ratner has explained, the use of direct address indicates Turner's self-isolation and confinement. It also unites the character as both witness and participant, as both observer of his own actions and actor in the unfolding drama that is the consequences of those actions. But it also, as Pearce points out, restricts the focus of the book to Turner's own monologue: "The 'true confession' always locates the fault within the heroine and never within the society that produced the conditions for her fall" (Pearce, 38). Decides Pearce, "The fault lies not in the social structure but within Nat's mind" (Pearce, 40). As John Gardner sees the first-person narrator, it "restricts character development" and in effect reproduces the experience of all of us "living in the first person because we're all in some sense monsters, trapped in our own language and habits of emotion."[19]

Turner's narration does limit the scope of the novel, but it doesn't undermine the social structure of which he is a part. If anything, Turner makes quite clear his experiences as a black slave in a racist society, and we as readers can see the experience of his isolation as a product of that very system. First-person narrations do not necessarily restrict the faults to the self alone, even though such narrations do devise elaborate schemes for self-justification and excuse. Perhaps the Freudian threads do undermine the missionary's commitment. A prophet, after all, can be no prophet when confined to the country of his own ego. We watch Turner consciously cloaking himself in mystery rather than being the enigmatic focus of some wider mystery.

The problem, however, is still one of distance. It is one thing for Turner to think he's achieved redemption at the end of the novel. It's another for Styron to think so. What Styron has become confused about or been unable to distance himself far enough from is his conception of Nat Turner and Nat Turner's conception of himself. For Styron to think of the structure of the book as a religious allegory, and for Turner to think of the end of his life in exactly the same terms, won't wash. Turner's redemption, as Turner tells it, is too self-serving and too filled with ironies for us to buy it completely. And yet Styron wants us to. Perhaps Styron's drive to reconcile the ambivalences of the character and the novel has directed him to sacrifice distance for identity. His attempts to do so end the novel on a specious and phony note.

Yet even with these problems intact, *The Confessions of Nat Turner* remains a powerful novel in its own right. The personal and racist issues that weaken the revolutionary "purity" of Turner's purpose also humanize the character and make of him a flesh-and-blood creature. The novel, which begins after the revolt has failed, returns to the personal development that took place to produce the need for that revolt, and then returns to Turner's execution, creates the full arc of meditation on history and event that Styron wished to achieve. With history as a guide, in both its details and its broad outline, in particular the history in Gray's *Confession,* Styron had managed to extricate himself from the stasis of self-encapsulation that paralyzed his first three fictions. In writing this novel he had both consciously and unconsciously confessed his own complicity in the twisted history of black and white that plagues all of us, and in doing so in 1967 had written the best novel of his career.

Chapter Seven
Sophie's Choice:
Styron's Heart of Darkness

In her book on the role of historical consciousness in American romance, Emily Miller Budick maintains that such consciousness provides the necessary antidote to America's self-absorption with its own biblical and prophetic paradigms.[1] America's sense of itself, at least in much American fiction, appears to revel in its own self-encapsulation, convinced it can free itself from history, chart its own course, be forever self-reliant, and triumph in its own mythical reenactments of eternal progress and self-making. Such a self-absorbed view can, of course, lead to disaster, wherein the self plays God and sees the world as only one more self-projection of its own anxieties and repressions. It is with this vision of self-encapsulation that Styron has been consistently saddled, and in *Sophie's Choice* he makes his most elaborate and successful fictional attempt to break free.

Within the novel several characters must acknowledge the past and their role in it in order to take their place in a world created by it. This acknowledging becomes the historical task of both the young and the older Stingo, the process on which Styron focuses his novel. It is also a process within which Sophie Zawistowska is imprisoned, but because of the nature of her involvement, her release from it, as we shall see, can be only in death.

In effect Styron must juggle the essential interrelation between the necessity of Sophie's suicide and the inevitability of Stingo's tragic understanding of her death and his complicity in it. And in witnessing the accomplishment of this feat, the reader must absorb and penetrate the explanations and experiences of the older Stingo, the twenty-two-year-old Stingo in 1947, Sophie's manner in revealing her past, and the nature of that incredible past in its own right. For our purposes, we can start with Sophie and her revelations and work outward in terms of their impact on the Stingo of 1947 and the older Stingo.

Sophie

Sophie's revelations provide the essentially Gothic structure of the novel. Hers is a process of revealing her role slowly, often seeking refuge in lies, il-

lusions, and inexplicable blanks in her testimony. Her confession relies on
the necessary repression of Gothic tales, hiding the awful truth as she goes
forward and making the revelation of that truth even more awful by the fact
that she feels she's had to repress and disown it for so long. The very act of
repression, of rhetorical foreplay, adds to the dark necessity of that truth's finally emerging in all its horror, made more so by her need to hide it for so
long.

Sophie's lying is no mere subterfuge. The lies keep her fragile equilibrium of consciousness intact, protecting her from the guilt that is consuming
her and from the inevitable death that will occur upon completion of her
confession. Once she reveals her secret, her most horrible choice, she in effect
signs her death warrant. She has lived to tell her tale, and the very telling of
it ensures her demise.

Of course Sophie's revelations raise interesting possibilities in the text,
since the older Stingo, who's telling the tale, already knows Sophie's
choices. He in effect is playing Sophie's game in writing the novel, delaying
the final revelation in the present as much as Sophie did in 1947. The reasons are several, as we shall see, but they do include Stingo's own sense of
guilt, his maintaining a fragile equilibrium in his own consciousness, and his
apparent need to focus more on the younger Stingo's loss of innocence and
Sophie's effect on him than on the horrible revelations of Sophie's life in and
of themselves.

The initial presence of Sophie in Stingo's life in 1947 is essentially an absence, for he first hears her involved in sexual revels with Nathan in the
room above his own before he actually sees her. She enters his life as a kind
of sexual siren, followed by Beethoven's Fourth Symphony, a musical motif
that will become more appropriate as the novel develops, since the resonant
interplay between sex, music, domination, and eventually death provides
the alarming and unrelenting subtext of Stingo's spiritual awakening.
Nathan's vicious verbal attack on Sophie follows the sex and music and
foreshadows the complex use and misuse of language throughout the novel.

Stingo's first sight of Sophie suggests Edgar Allan Poe's infatuation
with doomed and beautiful women. She reminds him of Maria Hunt, the
girl he knew from Virginia who had committed suicide in New York, and
convinces him that Sophie was already doomed. Already Stingo sees
Sophie in distress, presented as she is as a mixture of candor, passion, grief,
and woe. Her sickly emaciation suggests that she is already half-ghostlike,
a Poesque wraith on the verge of dissolution. Stingo's instant infatuation
with her also suggests his own morbid fascination with sex and death in
Poesque terms and reveals a kind of self-projection that bodes ill.

At the same time, in viewing Nathan as Sophie's evil guardian, Stingo sets himself up as a kind of hero in a sentimental romance. He will be the knight to rescue this fair, emaciated maid from the demonic dragon and in doing so will also satisfy his raging, unfulfilled lust. And yet beneath this sentimental stereotype, he is aware that Sophie remains "a cluster of contradictions" (*SC*, 265), filled with inexplicable glimpses of violence, joy, a kind of willfully submissive self-destruction, and power. He learns that she can stand up to Nathan, who has both rescued and attacked her in the past, and transform him. Such contradictions, with their demonic overtones, fascinate Stingo, and he vows to pursue them to their mysterious source.

Throughout the novel Sophie narrates six tales of revelation, each with its own self-image and each accompanied by the choices she has made or refused to make. As the tales appear, her sense of guilt and complicity begins to overcome and imprison her to such an extent that the reader begins to realize how fraught with danger her ultimate revelations—and choices—may be. Briefly and in the order of their telling, these tales include her false re-creation of life in Cracow (chapter 4); her capture and consignment to Auschwitz on 1 April 1943 (6); her involvement with Rudolf Hoss at Auschwitz (9, 10, and half of 11); her difficult involvements with a lover in Warsaw, Wanda, and the resistance movement (12); a more splintered version of her relationship with Walter Durrfeld in Cracow in 1937 and at Auschwitz (13); and finally her more convoluted involvement with Wanda in Warsaw and the horror of Eva's death at Auschwitz (15).

In each tale a choice is made or evaded. In Cracow, Sophie paints a picture of urban pastoral, an ultimately civilized life that suddenly is destroyed from without. The choices have not been hers. In the second tale she had stolen a ham to take to her mother, who is ill with tuberculosis, and is apprehended by the Nazis. In the third tale Sophie chooses to try to seduce Rudolf Hoss in order to get out of Auschwitz or at least to see or try to save her son, Jan. In her fourth disclosure to Stingo she refuses to join the resistance movement led by Wanda, since she feels that as a mother she has responsibilities enough in trying to support her children. In the fifth incarnation of her past she chooses at Auschwitz to try to steal a radio for Wanda and the resistance movement. And in the final tale she reveals her choice in helping to get guns for Wanda in Warsaw and in sacrificing her daughter to Jemand von Niemand's horrible offer.

At first Sophie presents her civilized life in Cracow as if it were ideal. Her father is a good man; both he and her husband, Kazik, are professors at the university; and her mother plays the piano. Music infiltrates this entire presentation of an urban pastoral existence. Sophie herself becomes the civilized innocent, a product of a cultured, faraway Europe that has been lost. In such a world the Nazis are the simple aggressors. They have ravaged and destroyed such an idyllic past. And in the Nazis' doing so the war and the displaced persons camp have left Sophie beyond feeling, as ravaged as that prewar landscape.

Guilt first emerges here, and it is defined in terms of Sophie's being unable to say farewell to her good father and husband, who had been rounded up, deported, and murdered by the Nazis, and in her own fortunate survival. Her loss of faith relies on the knowledge that God "could permit the people I loved to be killed and let me live with such guilt." She feels that "my eyes will never, never again see God" (*SC*, 103–4).

Styron juxtaposes this tale of the evil Nazis' rape of Cracow and European civilization with that of Sophie's rebirth in Brooklyn, her work for Dr. Hyman Blackstock, her glorying in music on the radio and concerts—music links her to that sad, idyllic past—her free English classes at Brooklyn College, and her reading Dos Passos and Wolfe. And yet the digital rape on the subway nearly capsizes her, violating her new, fragile sense of self-sufficiency and plunging her again into the nightmare of rape and violation that has been her incarnation of her Nazi-haunted past. Both Mozart on the radio and Dr. Blackstock help to comfort her, but it is Nathan who comes to the rescue when she passes out in the library. The innocent victim of rape in the past and present collapses when the two eras seem to be horribly reduplicating each other.

Sophie's self-image as pure victim underlies her second tale about her arrival at Auschwitz. Her crime of stealing a ham seems absurd in terms of its punishment. We learn that she spent twenty months incarcerated and that Auschwitz was the labor camp and Birkenau the place for extermination. There are hints of an involvement with Rudolf Hoss, but these are submerged in her representation of herself as a victim of the Nazi plague.

And yet Sophie's guilt hints at a self-loathing that seems out of proportion to the events she's describing. Stingo describes her love of Nathan as "dementia," and her tales take on a quality that is "secretive to the point of obsession" (*SC*, 177). It is Nathan who questions her reassessments of the past by hounding her with unanswered questions: "Tell me why it is . . . that *you* inhabit the land of the living. . . . Did the same anti-Semitism for which Poland has gained such world-wide renown—did a similar anti-Semitism guide your own destiny, help you along, *protect* you? . . . *Explanation, please!*" (*SC*, 254–55).

A major shift occurs in the novel when Sophie acknowledges her role as that of an accomplice within the larger role of victim. On the verge of her third tale, the one about her attempts to seduce Rudolf Hoss, Sophie reveals that she had been "both victim and accomplice, accessory—however haphazard and ambiguous and uncalculating her design"—and that this role involved playing up to Hoss as "an obsessed and poisonous anti-Semite—a passionate, avid, tediously single-minded hater of Jews" (*SC*, 266). It is also in this tale that Sophie's father is revealed as the rabid, pamphlet-publishing anti-Semite, proclaiming the necessity of Vernichtung, or extermination of the Jews. Stingo chalks the first portrait of Sophie's father up to "another fantasy served up to provide a frail barrier, a hopeless and crumbly line of defense between those she cared for, like myself, and her smothering guilt" (*SC*, 289).

The truth of Sophie's relationship with her father and with Hoss increases the recognition of her guilt and self-loathing. Despite being shocked by her father's views, she serves him faithfully, and with Kazik, helps distribute his pamphlets. She had also transcribed her father's dictation and acknowledges her total subservience to him and his wishes. This surrender to his work and personality may have been due to her Polish Catholicism, with its patriarchal veneration and obeisance, but it reveals a Sophie so subservient to this fealty that it raises darker questions about her attraction to Nazism as a kind of patriarchal worship. It is no wonder that her sense of guilt expands with the telling of this third tale: "This guilt is something I cannot get rid of and I think I never will" (*SC*, 349).

Such darker revelations underwrite Sophie's sense that she has been abandoned by God. And while she is relating this third tale to Stingo, she has also been abandoned by Nathan. In such a state she tells of the lesbian attack in Haus Hoss by the housekeeper Wilhelmine, of her showing her father's pamphlet to Hoss to assure him of her rabid anti-Semitism, and of the deal she hopes to make with Hoss to at least release Jan into the Lebensborn program, the Germans' systematized breeding program. As her present with Nathan collapses—and it, too, is one more sadomasochistic relationship, repeating her submission to patriarchal figures in the past—the past begins to overwhelm her.

It is then that Sophie reveals to Stingo Nathan's use of drugs and his attempt to initiate a suicide pact between the two of them after a humiliating episode of fellatio and kicking. This suicide attempt had followed an eruption of Nathan's jealousy at seeing Dr. Blackstock hug her, overwrought as Blackstock had become by the sudden death by decapitation of his wife. The demonic past foreshadows the demonic present, and in Sophie's nightmarish world of guilt and domination—both in the past and in the present—such parallels are so strong that we become aware she cannot possibly escape from them.

In such an atmosphere Sophie's tales begin to splinter in her telling of them, as past and present inexorably begin to repeat each other. In the fourth tale Sophie rejects involving herself with Wanda in the resistance, maintaining that she is a mother and daughter with two children and her own mother to provide for and that she is basically a self-effacing, very devout Catholic girl who should remain "stainless, inaccessible, uninvolved" (*SC,* 459). Such a self-image suggests the urban pastoral of Cracow once again and seems to be an attempt by Sophie to pull herself back together to restore herself after the yawning abyss of guilt and complicity revealed by her true relationships with her father and Hoss. The tale reveals her involvement with her young lover, Jozef, the executioner of Poles who betrayed Jews, a relationship that leads her to his sister Wanda and the politics of resistance.

As if trying to atone for her father's views, Sophie wants to keep herself aloof from involvements of all kinds, but fate intervenes and imprisons her with members of the resistance, including Wanda, on the way to Auschwitz. In 1947, while telling this tale, Sophie begins to drink excessively, reveals in her bitterness that "[a]ll my childhood, all my life I really hated Jews" (*SC,* 430), and attempts to drown herself. In this she provides Stingo with his only real attempt at rescuing her.

The web of complicity and self-deception widens in the fifth tale, as Sophie reveals her attraction to Walter Durrfeld, one more patriarchal figure, who turns out to be a German industrialist whom she first met in Cracow in 1937 and who turns up at Auschwitz to see Hoss and demand more Jewish workers for the cause. Her first "spasm of adulterous guilt" (*SC,* 472) in 1937 blossoms into blasphemy and suicide in the telling of the tale: "After Auschwitz, I didn't believe in God or if He existed. . . . I would commit my suicide in His church, on sacred ground" (*SC,* 500). In the course of this story we learn of Sophie's joining the resistance in trying to smuggle a radio belonging to Emmi Hoss (Hoss's young daughter), of Wanda's advising her to try to seduce Hoss as quickly as possible, and of Hoss's unwillingness to let Sophie see Jan, promising that he'll place the boy in the Lebensborn program. It is Wanda who tells Sophie that she has seen Jan later in the camp. Hoss has done nothing. Sophie is returned to the barracks for fifteen more months, five of which are spent in Birkenau, and Hoss leaves for Berlin.

In the final tale and in Stingo's and Sophie's final flight from Nathan on the way to Virginia, the horrifying and unbreakable cycle of guilt recurs.

Sophie acknowledges her having helped Wanda's gunrunning in Warsaw before Auschwitz and reveals the choice Von Niemand forced her to make in terms of her children's lives. Her sacrifice of Eva follows a deadly pattern, since once again a female has been delivered up to the deadly patriarchal host—the paradigm that underlies all of Sophie's horrifying past and present.

As a result, Sophie's guilt is total. She views herself as a coward who has been "turned to stone" (*SC*, 601), a final self-image that foreshadows her own death. She reveals that she often hoped that if the Nazis focused on the Jews as scapegoats, she could remain safe. She discloses lesbian episodes with Wanda and Wanda's bitter speech that cruelty leads only to further cruelty, not to some transcendent Christian notion of suffering and sacrifice. Sophie sees herself in the worst possible light: "I was a filthy *collaboratrice,* that I done everything that was bad just to save myself. . . . Oh, Stingo, I can't stand living with these things!" (*SC*, 554). Mesmerized by yet one final patriarchal oppressor, Sophie returns to die with Nathan, leaving her suicide note for Stingo: "I love Nathan but now feel this Hate of Life and God. FUCK God and all his Hande Werk. And Life too. And even what remain of Love" (*SC*, 607).

For Sophie, doomed from the beginning, only death and the completion of her revelations can release her from a self-encapsulation so eroded and undermined by guilt and despair. She has reconstructed a past that parallels the same sexual and suicidal patterns of her present, one feeding the other so completely that there can be no way out in life. Repression has kept her sane. Revelation kills her. And the effects of her death, the role that history plays in an individual's identity, and the horrors of her revealed existence are left for Stingo to try to understand.

Nathan

Perhaps the weakest or most improbable character in *Sophie's Choice* is Nathan Landau. He is the least realistic character, probably because he is conceived with a definite role to play: the demonic catalyst almost paralyzed by contradictions and shifting sensibilities within the dynamics of Sophie's confessions and Stingo's pursuit of them. "I wanted [Nathan] to be Sophie's destiny," Styron admitted in 1981, "her last executioner. The process of Sophie's destruction began at Auschwitz; Nathan completed it in Brooklyn" (Braudeau, 248).

Nathan has too many roles to play, from virulent anti-Nazi to romantic seducer, from sexual demon to brilliant biologist, from Sophie's rescuer and executioner to prescient prophet and dazzling entertainer—all of which boil down to the fact that he is clinically mad, a diagnosed schizophrenic. Whatever his position may be on anything, it is finally discovered as one more facet both of his manic-depression and his schizoid madness, a fact that may reveal Styron's more clinical assumptions about what lay at the heart of much of the Nazi-haunted past both in its attraction at the time and in its demonic solutions for so many victimizers and victims. Nathan's madness may be the final outcome of Sophie's needs as well, a culmination of similar states in the characters of Sophie's father, Kazik, Durrfeld, and Hoss. But in any case Nathan is so slippery and unreliable that his role as a demonic catalyst and Gothic gargoyle often overpowers his believability as a character.

Nathan's most mercurial and perhaps most successful role is that of Sophie's lover and executioner. He is a remarkable sexual athlete, fueled by a vicious jealousy and need to dominate. His rescuing of Sophie easily degenerates into his need to possess and dominate her. As a Jew he is understandably affected—at a party in the novel—by Harold Schoenthal's discussion of Polish anti-Semitism and the inability of Jews to be safe anywhere, and recognizing Sophie's non-Jewish Polish background, Nathan maliciously taunts her about how she was able to survive.

There is much in this aspect of Nathan that suggests more the monster or golem than the New York Jew, and critics have questioned the depth of his Jewishness and Styron's use of it. It does seem that his executioner's role transcends his background, although his being Jewish—and Sophie's not being Jewish—adds levels of irony to his role in her doom. Allen Rosenfeld's description of Nathan as an odd mixture of black potency and Jewish diabolism points more to the role Nathan is saddled with than to any anti-Semitic perspective on Styron's part. Nathan's vanishing from the text between chapters 9 and 13 indicates perhaps that Styron must get him out of the way to focus on Sophie's confessions and Stingo's pursuit of them, before bringing him back to complete his demonic role as executioner.

Nathan's least successful incarnation resides in Stingo's overzealous glorification of him, a kind of spiritual and physical seduction that we will examine more closely in the discussion later of the Stingo of 1947. Stingo has all kinds of reasons for worshiping Nathan in his morbid mix of a southerner's conjuring up of a New York Jew, his own unresolved oedipal tensions, and his passive attitude toward Nathan's shenanigans, but Stingo's description of Nathan never seems to match our image of him. Stingo spends so much time telling us how great Nathan is that we can easily see the discrepancy between his incarnation of Nathan and the

Nathan who actually performs and attacks. The burden of the highly romantic and wildly complimentary description that Stingo heaps upon
Nathan cannot possibly be carried by any character in a novel, unless that
character is kept at some mysterious distance, not seen up close. The
reader in effect sees too much of Nathan's downright viciousness to feel
satisfied with Stingo's tortuous apologies for and celebrations of him.

Nathan may look like John Garfield, but do we ever really see him as
Stingo does, as "part magic entertainer, part big brother, confidant and guru
[with] the depth of a masterful performer" (*SC*, 222)? Is he really "a
polymath—one who knows a great deal about almost everything" (*SC*,
224)? If he is indeed Stingo's "embodiment of everything I deemed attrac-
tive and even envied in a human being" (*SC*, 225), then isn't Stingo, too,
mesmerized by the kind of male domination that is grossly exaggerated in
Nazi-swaggering attacks on submissive and "doomed" women? Can all the
alchemy in the world and all the "dazzling invention" override the viciousness that Nathan reveals in his relationship with Sophie, even if we grant
that he is being victimized by "some transcendent desperation" (*SC*, 89)?
The demonic incarnation hits closer to home—we see Nathan in his demonic roles—and the image of the seductive dazzler fails to shake that first
revelation of his savage and practically demented character.

Even a realistic point of view cannot really salvage Nathan outside of
Stingo's overarching worship of him. The moody biologist, creating a "ho-
munculus" and possible cure for cancer, seems forced and uncertain. Nathan
tells us of his breakthroughs, and it is difficult to buy them. He remains
"emotionally jazzed up" (*SC*, 245) from our first impressions of him, and
his attacks on Sophie and Stingo, his leaps from sex to rage, his giddy Lenny
Bruce routines, and his wilder improvisations come to appear vicious and
silly. We long for a clearer explanation of him, and when we find out about
the headaches, the drugs, and the final revelation from his brother Larry
that he is simply mad, he deflates in front of our eyes as a sick soul who has
no moral authority whatsoever. How could Stingo have been so deceived?

And yet in the scheme of things Nathan operates as an elusive catalyst,
even if he does seem more the unrealistic dragon of romance than a character in a novel. As the "wicked genie" guarding the distraught maiden, he is
there for the knight to overpower and outwit. The fact that Nathan "wins"
underscores the demonic guilt at the center of Sophie's fate. He has become
the final projection of her submissive sacrifice to one more crazed and demented father figure, and in that fatal attraction he brings the novel to its
dark conclusion, acting to the end more as the driven demon in Sophie's
Gothic universe than as a realistic character in the Brooklyn of 1947.

Stingo

"Call me Stingo" begins the second paragraph of *Sophie's Choice,* a phrase filled with the resonance of Melville's orphaned outcast Ishmael. "In those days," begins the first, placing the nicknamed Stingo as a twenty-two-year-old virgin in 1947, the proverbial American innocent about to undergo a spiritual and sexual quest, both terms of which seem almost grotesquely intermixed in the mind of our horny hero. And suddenly in a boardinghouse in Brooklyn he is faced with a strange woman and her strange relationship with a strange man, a circumstance automatically fascinating to the mind of a would-be writer who also sees himself as "another lean and lonesome young Southerner wandering amid the Kingdom of the Jews" (*SC,* 1).

Stingo is immediately attracted to Sophie and to the "exotic" Jew Nathan, and their raucous lovemaking forces him "into this position of lubricious curiosity [trapped as he is in] an episode of pornographic eavesdropping. . . . I am not by nature a snoop; but the very proximity of the two lovers . . . made it impossible for me to avoid trying to discover their identity" (*SC,* 46). In his eyes both Jews and southerners have been caught up by that "rock-hard encounter with the anguish of Abraham and Moses' stupendous quest," and his own present quest is now made clear: "Sophie and Nathan had quite simply laid siege to my imagination" (*SC,* 68).

At first Stingo seems almost a type, the American innocent suffering in his "morbid and solitary period" as a "crazy hermit," lonely, claustrophobic, unaware of the consequences of love and death, experiencing only that certain "hollowness" of the self-encapsulated Styron character we've come to know so well. He seems at times almost willfully innocent, cocooned in his "smug and airless self-deprivation" (*SC,* 29), as if he were clinging to some role to avoid commitment and all the consequences that come with it. By the time near the end of the novel when he laments, *"God in heaven!* Was I fated to go through life a gullible and simple-minded waif, with those whom I cared for the most forever pulling the wool over my eyes?" (*SC* 517), we begin to wonder if perhaps he is protesting too much, relying on his "innocence" almost as an excuse to justify his errors of judgment and his often-evasive actions.

Stingo's is that brand of "radical innocence" which Ihab Hassan explored in his 1961 book on the subject, conjuring up a paradigm of an American type that Styron has never been able to relinquish. Such an "innocent" recoils from experience, as if such recoil were "one of the resources of its awareness, a strategy of its *will.*"[2] It seems one more myth lifted out of American history to be examined under glass in a kind of paradigmatic purity, a state that denies the very sense of history it must learn to deal with in order to be "initiated" into adulthood. Such a self-encapsulating notion has always fit many of Styron's fictions and seems at times very much a product of the New Criticism of the 1950s.

Styron fleshes out this paradigm with other recognizable characteristics, some more a development of the "unbuttoned" fiction of the 1960s and 1970s and some part and parcel of the innocent's baggage. Stingo describes himself as a "hopelessly old-fashioned romantic," at one with his naïveté, and as in the bulk of Styron's fiction he also sees himself as "fortune's darling" (*SC*, 27). Stingo's self is somehow special, despite the stereotypical attributes with which he describes that self, and he views his failure to conform to the social structure at McGraw-Hill as a triumph of the self over a "vast and soulless empire" (*SC*, 6). He had been a marine like his senior editor's son, but that son, Eddie Farrell, had been killed, perhaps the first of others' sacrifices for Stingo's fortunate initiation into the mysteries of life. At the same time he recognizes the unmitigated agony of his "stallionoid condition" (*SC*, 200), which he barely manages to control by an uneasy reliance on his wavering Presbyterian ethics.

Stingo is also a nascent writer, suffering from "Wolfe-worship," and his love of language incarnates a complex substitute for and an evasion and celebration of the erotic. For him "the written word . . . was so excitable that it verged on the erotic" (*SC*, 12). In fact when Stingo writes and paces "my cell distractedly, uttering soft meaningless vocables to the air as I struggled with the prose rhythms," he has to "[fight] back the desolate urge to masturbate that for some reason always accompanied this task" (*SC*, 14). The relationship between sex and language will grow into a complicated vision in the novel itself, as we shall see, a recognition Styron already makes clear at the very beginning.

Stingo's own style resonates with inflated Gothic rhetoric, the extravagent tropes of the dark, overheated romantic. His lust is "something prehensile, a groping snout of desire, slithering down the begrimed walls of the wretched old building, uncoiling itself . . . serpentine" (*SC*, 15), the original snake in Eden. And his description of "the creative heat which at eighteen had nearly consumed me with its gorgeous, relentless flame" extends the imagery of Promethean fire to its present diminishment in the older Stingo, since it "had flickered out to a dim pilot light registering little more than a token glow in my breast" (*SC*, 1). He delights in the Keatsian assonance of his prose as he describes "the spring wind whistl[ing] with the noise of demons around McGraw-Hill's green indifferent eaves" (*SC*, 28). At this point in his young life, his rhetoric is as much a smokescreen, a kind of masturbatory incantation, as it is a wrestling with real dilemmas, and the reader must keep an eye out to see how or if it changes as Stingo's awareness of life around him assuredly does.

In terms of these early characteristics—Stingo's loneliness and isolation, his notion of being fortune's darling, his sexual obsessions, and his love for Gothic rhetoric—Styron deepens and develops the character of Stingo as the novel develops. Stingo's isolation becomes pathological; he so hungers for friendship that he seems poised to grasp at any neighboring straw. His "self-flagellating withdrawal" (*SC*, 134), partaking of a monklike preoccupation with denied sexuality, also reveals his attraction to morbid themes, to "suicide, rape, murder, military life, marriage, slavery" (*SC*, 131). As a southerner in the mysterious North he is more than ripe for becoming involved with the beautiful and doomed Sophie.

Stingo's good fortune is closely linked to America's in 1947, as he becomes aware how much his innocence is a product of time and place: "*God*, I thought, what Americans had been spared in our era, after all" (*SC*, 240). And he comes to believe in his own intuitive reasons for believing sections of Sophie's story as she reveals her terrible past. Part of his good fortune is being able to know what he wants: to write a novel, to get to know Sophie and Nathan, to experience once and for all sexual fulfillment.

A good basis for Stingo's outlook stems from his image of his father, the decent southern liberal, the antislavery Virginia gentleman, the man who in his "simple eloquence" can comment on old-fashioned virtues and vices. Stingo's Chesterfieldian heritage, when it clashes with a cabdriver over a nickel in New York, makes the fact much clearer to Stingo that here is a decent guide, however the times may have surpassed his reckoning of them, whose largeness of vision he can take comfort in. Stingo clings to his southern heritage out of nostalgia and need perhaps, but it is there to rely on and to see him through, "as uncomplicated as an abiding belief in good manners and public decency" (*SC*, 357).

Sex dominates Stingo's waking and sleeping hours, obsessed as he is with his virginity, which strikes him, in all his rhetorical giddiness, as his own abiding Golgotha. But it is more than sex that mesmerizes him: "With me the most memorable of dreams, the ones that have achieved that haunting reality so intense as to be seemingly bound up in the metaphysical, have dealt with either sex or death" (*SC*, 54). In the case of Maria Hunt, a suicide in Manhattan and former friend from Virginia, sex and death seem ineradicably intertwined, a dark conflagration in his own mind engendered perhaps by his morbidity and his hermitlike isolation. Sophie comes to embody his Poesque fixation with sex and death in a manner that will illuminate

Styron's development of the intermixture of them both with language, the self, and one's own twentieth-century identity.

Stingo's sense of sex and language continues to develop as well. His biblical, Gothic-romantic rhetoric, which, as we shall see, is often undercut by the older Stingo, feeds both his erotic need for words and his linguistic expressions of sex. Words can inflame his lust, as witnessed in his slang-ridden conversations with Leslie Lapidus, a Jewish girl he meets in New York. When it comes to language, Lapidus shows none of the inhibitions Stingo reveals. Unfortunately, he discovers too late that "her sex life is wholly centered in her tongue" (*SC,* 214), but this discovery reveals to him how quickly he can be possessed by language, as Sophie suggests Faulkner must have been, possessed by the "real thing." At the same time, Stingo recognizes that language can also be used to repress, "that the repressiveness of a society in general is directly proportional to its harsh repressions of sexual language" (*SC,* 216). Even sexual language can be used to repress the "real thing." And the older Stingo realizes how words can penetrate, how they can assist both a spiritual and a sexual quest, the latter seemingly uppermost in the younger Stingo's mind, the former in the older's. In both cases penetration of a soul or body provides the key, and language provides the medium of unlocking the door.

Alongside Stingo's isolation, good fortune, sexual obsessions, and rhetorical forays, Styron also darkens and deepens his hero's character. Guilt, while nowhere near as smothering or as destructive as it is in Sophie's life, haunts Stingo's soul. The money he has been given to survive in New York has come from the sale of a slave, ironically named Artiste, who was sold after having been charged with making sexual advances, which allegations proved to be false, to a white woman. Slavery of course fills Stingo with guilt, as do the tales of Bobby Weed and Theodore Bilbo, with their revelations of murder and political racism. Stingo is often an easy target for Nathan's antisouthern tirades and realizes, as Styron did, that in the future he would have to confront Nat Turner and the South's racist past in order to "make him mine, and re-create him for the world" (*SC,* 514). Such racist guilt is complicated also by the "sexual moonscape" of 1947 and its accompanying puritanical inhibitions, as well as by Stingo's momentary desertion of his dying mother.

Stingo cannot forgive himself for the afternoon when, at age twelve, he abandoned his mother, ravaged by the cancer that would kill her, and went off for a ride with a schoolmate. He returned to find his mother shivering, since it had been his job to keep the fire in the fireplace burning. He cannot forget her eyes or, more to the point, "the *swiftness* of [her] turning away which would thereafter define my guilt"; he has come to believe that "my crime was ultimately beyond expiation, for in my mind it would inescapably and always be entangled in the sordid animal fact of my mother's death" (*SC*, 361). Such guilt will never leave him, nor will his sense of failing her, an incident that keenly foreshadows his dealings with Sophie. He continues to be haunted by a nightmare in which he "caught sight of the open coffin . . . then saw my mother's shrunken, cancer-ravaged face twist toward me . . . and gaze at me beseechingly through eyes filmed over with indescribable torture" (*SC*, 54). In Stingo's initial isolation and self-encapsulation, such nightmares never leave him.

Stingo's attraction to death and morbid mystery even infiltrates his attraction to Jews. He is drawn to "all that was isolate, mysterious and even supernatural about Jews and Jewry and their smoky, cabalistic religion" (*SC*, 196), as if half in love with easeful death, his own isolation projected onto an exotic world of "monotonous chants" and "rabbis in skullcaps moaning in a guttural tongue as they went about their savage rites—circumcising goats, burning oxen, disemboweling newborn lambs" (*SC*, 198). For Stingo, Jews incarnate the dark and mysterious in the gloomy darkness of their synagogues, a reflection of his own dark enchantments.

Slowly his own obsession with Sophie develops into a kind of demonic possession, as if he wants to sacrifice himself up to some dark mystery beyond his self-encapsulated control, whether it is sex, death, or language or, in fact, a compulsive combination of all three. At first Stingo envisions himself as the gallant knight come to rescue Sophie from the clutches of Nathan, the "wicked genie." " 'Love *me!* Love life!' " Stingo shouts in his shower to himself, "while I lathered my crotch" (*SC*, 425). But then fate seems to take over, as if in projecting his lust for dark mysteries and forces, he has half-created a Gothic demon that has taken possession of him. He suffers doubts about "getting sucked toward the epicenter of such a volatile, destructive relationship" (*SC*, 72)—the phrase resonates with sexual allusions and Sophie's half-attraction to Nazism—yet acknowledges, "I was fated to get ensnared, like some hapless June bug, in the incredible spider's nest of emotions that made up the relation between Sophie and Nathan" (*SC*, 104).

Stingo's haplessness is no mere innocent state; his very soul has encouraged the growth of and entrapment within that "incredible spider's nest of emotions," as much as it has contributed to the "something sick, self-flagellating in my withdrawal from people into a world of fantasy and loneliness" (*SC*, 134). With such forces released, Stingo's "Sophiemania" overpowers him, and in the presence of Sophie and Nathan, "I felt close to total salvation" (*SC*, 80).

There is a part of the virginal Stingo that longs to be seduced, whether it be by Sophie or by Nathan, by language or by visions of death and destruction. He may regard himself at first as a pawn, misguided by external masquerades, but he willfully ignores the storm warnings in Nathan's outbursts and evades or eradicates those warnings when Nathan returns to "normal." Stingo, as many an American hero before him, also has a tendency to polarize his perspective; he chooses to see the world in terms of the simplistic (and one could say Puritan) categories of either/or rather than the more complex interminglings of both/and. Thus to continue Nathan's seduction of him—or his own seduction of himself at the hands of the Nathan he has himself conjured up—he continues to ignore the bad in order to celebrate the good, to repress the golem and applaud the dazzling performer.

Stingo later realizes that he finally must encounter his "misgivings and suspicions which up until now I had successfully repressed" (*SC*, 519). It's an almost-classic case of ambivalence wherein in repressing his suspicions, in order to get on with his necessary reconciliations with Nathan, those suspicions, "the intensity of a buried emotion one has felt toward another person—a repressed animus or a wild love—comes heaving to the surface of consciousness with immediate clarity; sometimes it is like a bodily cataclysm, ever unforgettable" (*SC*, 290). And since repression plays its very definite role in confessions·in general and the Gothic romance/novel in particular, it is necessary that Stingo should harbor them.

Stingo's euphoric panegyric in his descriptions of Nathan have already been touched upon, but it does carry with it the darker aspects of Stingo's celebration of the sinister, something to which he is drawn but something which must lie outside himself, as if he can enjoy it only voyeuristically, the willful innocent clutching his cocoon of identity like an amorphous sea creature in its shell. Stingo loves the riddle and the mystery, the darkness of his fantasies about Jews, and in such a shadow Nathan emerges as Stingo's demonic alter ego. Nathan, after all, has rescued Sophie. Stingo has been unable to rescue his mother or Maria Hunt. The decisive, however schizophrenic, Nathan acts, whereas Stingo can only react and in doing so longs to be seduced by the dazzling actor, if only to reveal his own self-projected world of further enigmas and darker mysteries. Homoerotic possibilities hover in such dark corridors of the spirit and suggest that all the darkness may be a smokescreen repressing deeper sexual needs, a mask to worship in order to avoid the face beneath.

Sex and death, both in dreams and deeds, haunt Stingo's consciousness throughout the novel. He recognizes that he is drawn to "brutality and de-spairing tenderness and perverse eroticism and its stink of death" (*SC*, 425). His sex objects are dead women or at least those women who are sexually dead to him—Maria Hunt, Leslie Lapidus, Sophie Zawistowska. The novel bristles with scenes of fellatio, digital rape, "my first homosexual dream" (*SC*, 533), and blasphemous fornications, so much so that Mary Alice Grimball, the "whack-off artist," can say, "I was burnt so badly once" (*SC*, 531) without apparent irony in a novel within which Auschwitz emerges to overshadow everything else. The dead pile up rapidly: Eddie Farrell, Maria Hunt, Bobby Weed, Sophie's father and husband, Stingo's mother, Artiste, Nat Turner, Sylvia Blackstock, Jozef and Wanda, Eva, Jan, Sophie and Nathan. Death and sex intertwine. Sophie masturbates Stingo on the beach and tells her story of the dead Jozef. Stingo's and Sophie's last night to-gether, a cornucopia of omnivorous sexual frenzy, suggests the need for "car-nal oblivion [that may] beat back death" (*SC*, 603).

There is one other darker facet to Stingo's character, and that is the calcu-lating writer who's searching for a story to tell. He admits at first that he has "nothing to say" (*SC*, 132), that in him sensation precedes vision, sensibility precedes plot, and his sense of place precedes a definite story. But slowly he recognizes the "ghoulish opportunism" in the emergence of Sophie and her stories, much as he admits that Maria Hunt "had died just at that moment when I most needed that wondrous psychic jolt known as inspiration" (*SC*, 132). Maria's family can provide him with characters for his first novel, her doom reveal the hell of the bourgeois family life necessary for what in Styron's life became *Lie Down in Darkness*. In some instances Stingo notice-ably enjoys Sophie's sudden changes of mood; these provide fodder for his art. And he can compare the violence in him with that in Dostoyevsky's Raskolnikov or his own self-encapsulated journals unironically with André Gide's.

At one point Nathan informs Stingo that "Southern writing as a force is going to be over within a few years [and] you've got a lot of guts to be writ-ing in a worn-out tradition" (*SC*, 137). Not only is the tradition at stake here, but the older Stingo realizes that so was his own self: "I realize now how intensely discontented, rebellious and troubled I was at that age, but also how my writing had kept serious emotional distress safely at bay, in the sense that the novel I was working on served as a cathartic instrument through which I was able to discharge on paper many of my more vexing tensions and miseries" (*SC*, 535). His dying mother read books as a "nar-cotic" to combat the fact of her cancer. Here Stingo raises the same issue of evasion, coupled with his acknowledgment that his rhetoric was a kind of masturbatory discharge to keep "serious emotional distress"—serious sexual commitment?—"at bay."

Stingo wrestles with the task of writing and the guises of language. Words can be used to confront such symbolic characters as Nat Turner, to combat the kind of silence George Steiner, the literary critic, advocates, as we shall see in looking at the older Stingo. Words can evade and become a substitute for sexual experience and commitment: "I was simply not old sexy Stingo, and I had to be content with that fact. . . . I was a writer, an artist [and many great artists] had not allowed some misplaced notion of the primacy of the groin to subvert grander aims of beauty and truth" (*SC*, 218).

Words are necessary for survival. Sophie gets by at Auschwitz as a secretary, which places her on a rung above the "ordinary" inmate. Without words no quest is possible; like sex they can be used to penetrate experience, to tell stories. But words can also repress and disguise, as Stingo uses them in denying Nathan's darker side or as the superficially optimistic Reverend DeWitt hides behind them at Sophie's and Nathan's funeral. Theodore Bilbo dies of cancer of the mouth, a living metaphor for his own racist politics. This intricate complicity with language therefore both reveals and reveils Stingo's own complicities, beyond the American paradigm of "innocence," in terms of life's darker designs involving human submission and domination, sexual compulsions, and the lure of death.

Throughout the novel Stingo continues to make excuses for Nathan, forgiving him for and forgetting his outbursts, while the reader becomes more aware of Stingo's compulsion to do so. His own excuses—that he is too genteel or good mannered to recognize any real disorder in Nathan—begin to wear thin. And the apocalypse that he begins to expect, has in fact expected from the beginning, he also seems half in love with, as if hungering for some final explosion to jettison his timid soul from its shell of self-encapsulation.

The problematic finale of chapters 15 and 16, while in no way failing to sustain the book's jolting conclusions, does, however, raise questions about how much Stingo has learned and how much he is willing to act on that knowledge. Unlike the bleaker conclusions to *Lie Down in Darkness* and *The Long March,* these chapters suggest Cass Kinsolving's sudden resurrection at the hands of Luigi and Nat Turner's sudden apotheosis of love as redemption.

Stingo decides to take Sophie to Virginia with him and persuade her to marry him. And they will have to marry, because what would the neighbors think if they knew the couple were just living together in the farmhouse Stingo's father has offered to him? When Stingo raises the question of whether or not he's "willfully blind or dim-witted or both" (*SC*, 613), certainly one wonders. Does he really believe he can carry it off, after all that's happened? Or isn't this just one more evasion, one more refuge in escape, hoping for the kind of happy ending and ultimate reconciliation with Sophie that the novel up to this point has convinced us is impossible? How "innocent" can a twenty-two-year-old virgin be?

But Stingo goes on. He's convinced he can use Sophie for his book and establish himself as a writer. He tells her that she was just a victim of circumstances: "That camp made you behave in a different way than in the ordinary world. You told me yourself that you just couldn't judge what you did or what anyone else did in terms of accepted conduct" (*SC*, 554). Has he failed to hear what she's been telling him for hundreds of pages? Since Auschwitz made her do the things she did, does this fact excuse her? Once more has the "child" been forced to do something for which only the "parent" or patriarchal party (the Nazis, in this case) has the ultimate responsibility? Are the oedipal bonds loosening or tightening? Once again the oedipal encapsulation shrouds Stingo's notions: it's not your fault; you're not responsible; it's theirs, your father's, Hoss's, them.

Stingo tells us that he has a sense of the absurdity of things when he learns that on the day Sophie entered Auschwitz, he was eating bananas to gain weight to join the marines. But if he truly recognizes the absurd, why is he fleeing to a peanut farm in Virginia, oblivious to Sophie's confessions?

Sophie seems to realize how "innocent" Stingo remains. She wishes to confess everything, as if to break through his smug fantasies once and for all. She recognizes her role as an accomplice in her "crimes," that the mere notion of victimhood will not suffice. She disrupts Stingo's flight from reality by injecting Wanda's vision that everyone is a victim, that everyone is ultimately doomed, and that "adversity produces not understanding and compassion, but cruelty" (*SC*, 575). Yet Stingo presses on, convinced that even if Sophie will feel out of place in Virginia, "Southerners are the warmest and most *accepting* people in America, once they get to know you" (*SC*, 596). He realizes he may be "jabbering at Sophie with brainless unrestraint," but he persists, caught up in one more flight, one more attempt at evasion and escape.

At last he recognizes the fatal distance between them. Sophie still loves Nathan. But if, as he tells us, "I had identified so completely with Sophie that I felt Polish" (*SC*, 599), why should this realization come as such a shock? Such querulous questions are lost in the apotheosis of sex. Stingo's own quest for sexual conquest and experience has at last been answered. In a curious way, so has Sophie's. She vanishes the next morning, leaving him momentarily deflowered, triumphant, and without her to deal with.

And yet what does Stingo do? He decides to continue south, abandoning Sophie to Nathan, angry and jealous that she has chosen Nathan over him. He decides to forget her in one final fling at escape that suggests more of a pure and willful selfishness than it does an addled innocence. He seems to be brought to his senses during a "religious convulsion," after he's told us that he hates God as much as Sophie does, and he seems to take comfort in the "motherly" black woman and the "Book of Job." Since Stingo admits that "I had not been in any sense a godly-minded creature, and the Scriptures were always largely a literary convenience, supplying me with allusions and tag lines for the characters in my novel" (*SC*, 613), one isn't exactly certain how to react to this sudden "conversion," safely shared with a comforting black mother figure.

At the funeral of Sophie and Nathan, Stingo debunks the muddled eulogy of the Reverend DeWitt, with his "synthetically serene face" (*SC*, 619), and instead selects a poem by Emily Dickinson that, in terms of the plot, is far more appropriate. Nathan rescued Sophie at the library where she was searching for Dickinson's works when she fainted. Stingo then decides to sum up his experience. He believes that "*Someday I will understand Auschwitz*" (*SC*, 623), a notion that the older, wiser Stingo will openly reject. Then he decides to "let your love flow out on all living things," a sentimental notion that seems at odds with his initiation into the devastating mysteries of evil, death, sex, and loss. Taken together, these two lines recreate the very polarized perspective that Stingo began with: Auschwitz and love, death and rebirth. Two polarized opposites stare him in the face, unhealed, unreconciled. Is this perhaps the meaning of Styron's quotation from André Malraux, "I seek that essential region of the soul where absolute evil confronts brotherhood"?

Stingo's third attempt to sum up his experiences lies in his own lines of poetry: " 'Neath cold sand I dreamed of death / but woke at dawn to see / in glory, the bright, the morning star" (*SC*, 625). That same star all too swiftly revealed itself as well to Nat Turner, who on the day of his death willfully turned away from the darker mysteries of the doorless, windowless white sepulchre of his dreams and turned instead to his masturbatory celebration of love. Stingo, buried alive in sand on the beach overnight and suffering from Poesque dreams, "myself being split in twain by monstrous mechanisms" (*SC*, 625), yet wakens to a bright new morning, "blessing my resurrection." "This was not judgment day—only morning. Morning: excellent and fair," he intones, remembering Dickinson's verse (*SC*, 626).

Has Stingo undergone a "real" resurrection, or is this one more flight of fantasy, one more "tag line" to end his dark night of the soul and force the rebirth into morning? Sophie's death has proved to be his dream of death, from which he has been all too easily awakened. Has he shed his shell of self-encapsulated innocence or merely reconfirmed it all too willfully? The answer, I think, lies in the older Stingo's reactions to the tale about his younger self, a perspective that provides the kind of overview the novel needs to escape the "blind and dim-witted" conclusions of a twenty-two-year-old would-be writer. And it is that view which rescues the younger Stingo from the ineradicable self-encapsulation of so many of Styron's earlier characters.

Stingo and Sophie

Several critics have suggested that Stingo's story overwhelms and trivializes Sophie's, that his obsession with sex undercuts the tragic repercussions of her life and its effects on his. William Heath, for instance, suggests that "Styron makes the two tales compete with each other [and that] Stingo insists that his suffering must be taken as seriously as Sophie's."[3] To Heath, Stingo's personality and story "[seem] to be an ill-considered indulgence and a narcissistic attempt to sabotage Sophie's much more significant chronicle." Stingo's traits enable him "to exploit others, avoid unpleasant truths, and celebrate the imperial self" (*Heath,* 538, 545). For one thing, Heath seems to be criticizing another novel. *Sophie's Choice* is after all about the young—and older—Stingo coming to grips with Sophie's history, not mainly about Sophie. And for another, the connections between Stingo and Sophie are closer than Heath realizes.

Both Stingo and Sophie feel they are outsiders. Stingo longs to belong to the Hunnicutts' enchanted garden, filled with, in his imagination, celebrated and experienced writers. At the same time he is a southerner in New York, in many ways as strange an experience for him as it is for Sophie. She too has been on the outside of a garden looking in—the "enchanted bower" or sanctuary of Haus Hoss at Auschwitz—and she longs to enter it for her own necessary purposes. The southerner in the kingdom of the Jews and the Catholic Pole, the survivor of Auschwitz, in America: both these outsiders meet at Yetta's Pink Palace, her "Liberty Hall," as she describes it, in Brooklyn.

In many stories and myths, the crossroads is the potent place where anything can happen. As Chinua Achebe, the distinguished Nigerian writer, describes it, "[L]iving at the crossroads . . . is a very potent location—it's the intersection of things. The humans and the spirits meet at the cross-roads; the water and the land; the night and the day. These are very potent moments, so the crossroads is where people take their sacrifice, because they want this to get to the spirits. It's a place of opportunity—it's also very dangerous. And for me, this is where creativity exists, at these points of tension."[4] Yetta's Pink Palace suggests Hawthorne's "neutral territory" where Hawthorne's truth of the human heart can be explored. It is the center of Faulkner's art, that revelation that Faulkner described as "the human heart in conflict with itself."

The boardinghouse by its very nature provides a kind of sanctuary, a kind of "neutral territory" for migrants, strangers, and drifters. It is a place to cultivate new identities, full as it is of dislocation and uncertainty. For Sophie only death can give her the identity and peace she craves; too much history has happened to her. But for Stingo, the young American of 1947 and "fortunate" to be such, revelation and restoration of a kind are possible.

The older Stingo connects Sophie's Poland with Stingo's South and draws the parallels that the younger Stingo only senses "through Sophie's eyes and memory that summer" (*SC,* 301). While some of the parallels may be forced, uneasily aligned with the American habit of creating ahistorical connections in time and space and minimizing extraordinary differences and chasms of experience, still many of the broad parallels suggest kindred spirits: the racist past, the history of defeat, "pride in ancestry and family name . . . a poverty-ridden, agrarian, feudal society" (*SC,* 301). Another level of kinship between Stingo and Sophie comes into clearer focus here.

Both Stingo and Sophie love and crave music. It is Stingo's "reason for being" (*SC,* 140); it is Sophie's "life's blood" (*SC,* 565). She in fact wished to follow in her mother's footsteps and become a music teacher. Both Stingo and Sophie share Styron's love of classical music, and Styron shares Stingo's delight in "whispering melodiously (as I still do) the invented phrases and sentences" (*SC,* 133), the prose rhythms of his and Stingo's art.

As with so much in this resonant book, music has its darker side, its exclusion from life's pain, as both Sophie and Stingo come to recognize. Sophie "found she could not bear the contrast between the abstract yet immeasurable beauty of music and the almost touchable dimensions of her own aching despair" (*SC,* 112). Beethoven's Fourth Symphony is heard on WQXR during the tale of Nathan's rescuing Sophie and is played at one final reconciliation among the three characters, but Sophie and Nathan have also played it on their deathbed. Stingo's love of music culminates at one point in Bach's "Jesu, Joy of Man's Desiring," Cantata 47; it is also the last record on the player next to Sophie's and Nathan's deathbed. As Frederick

Karl suggests in relating Styron's use of music, throughout *Sophie's Choice,* to Thomas Mann's, here appears once again "the Mann thesis: that in man's highest gifts one can discover the greatest areas of evil, or that man's highest gifts lie closely associated with the lowest forms of human behavior" (Karl, 535). Music, after all, is like an idea: something about its beauty, however celebrated, remains inherently authoritarian and suspiciously inhuman.

Both Stingo and Sophie come to hate religion and Freudian psychology. Sophie feels that the loss of God is as fatal for her as the loss of music. She views God as a monster, and Stingo, however imprisoned in his residual Calvinism, proclaims, "I hate God, too!" (*SC,* 463). "Fuck God" becomes Sophie's final suicidal epithet, for as death claims her, she passes beyond Stingo's more evanescent declaration. And both berate the need for Freudian analysis, Stingo in his frustrating episode with Leslie Lapidus, Sophie in her disparagement of Nathan's friends who talk of suffering but have experienced none. In both instances of religion and psychology, specific dogmas are more or less rejected.

Both Stingo and Sophie love Nathan, and their love is riddled with anxieties, lack of self-esteem, and uncertain self-images. Sophie laments, "I deserve his abuse. I love him so!" (*SC,* 62). And Stingo goes out of his way to agree, dazzled by the very performer he needs to be dazzled by. Nathan and Stingo's and Sophie's convoluted relationship with him provide the dark fulcrum for their own coming together.

"Mothers and fathers—they're at the core of one's own life somehow. Or they can be" (*SC,* 564), Stingo suggests to Sophie at one point. And certainly the both of them suffer from Styron's oedipal self-encapsulations throughout the novel. Sophie's father is such an acknowledged tyrant and she is so utterly submissive to him that she explains, "All through this my father seemed to . . . *authorize* this horror, not only authorize it but *create* it in some way" (*SC,* 568). His complete domination of her and her need to appease and submit to him, to please him despite his demonic designs, overshadow all of Sophie's motives throughout the novel. How different from Stingo's father, that man of Chesterfieldian advice, good manners, and public decency. And yet in his own way Stingo submits to his father's largeness of vision, however much he can see that it no longer suits or describes the world in which he finds himself. In a way, both characters seek refuge in a father's authority to lessen their own guilts, but such oedipal nets only ensnare the shattered and crippled self-image.

Sophie's and Stingo's mothers were ill, and both deserted them in a fashion. Sophie was shipped off to Auschwitz. Stingo cannot let go the nightmare of his dead mother and the memory of his abandoning her that one afternoon to a cold room. In both instances, death and guilt play their ac-customed roles.

But the real connections between Sophie and Stingo emerge in their nightmares. In that border realm, that subconscious crossroads, they both dream of death, sex, and guilt in often ghastly incarnations. Stingo, in dreaming of sex, conjures up the dead Maria Hunt and then his mother's cancerous face, as if sexual possession for him inspires images of death and loss. He is first attracted to Sophie because of her passing resemblance to Maria Hunt, another crossroads where death and sex intermingle. Sophie's dreams of her father and of sex in church with Walter Durrfeld, perhaps the most disturbing nightmare in the novel, also conjure up images and circum-stances that are "violently, unequivocally and pleasurably erotic, so blasphe-mous and frightening" (*SC*, 490). Behind both characters lie unsettling dreamscapes filled with instances of submission and domination, erotic fan-tasies and the ever-present shadow of death. Is it any wonder "why [Sophie's] dream lover became so easily metamorphosed into the devil" (*SC*, 494)?

In an unpublished article, Daniel Ross explores the fact that both Sophie and Stingo have suffered the death of loved ones of the opposite sex, that both feel guilty for their inability to help such suffering loved ones as their mothers, Maria Hunt, Jan, and Eva.[5] Stingo's sexual anxieties involve his passivity with women; he wishes to rescue them, and yet he consistently fails them. He fears, having failed his mother and Maria Hunt, that he will fail Sophie as well. His obsessions with sex and death become relentlessly inter-twined. His saving Sophie from drowning is his only successful rescue, and he fails to save her from her suicide pact with Nathan.

Sophie remains dominated by her father, who seems to reemerge in the characters of Walter Durrfeld, Rudolf Hoss, and in many ways Nathan Landau. She was sexually attracted to Durrfeld, an instance that reveals her psychic complicity with Nazism and the Final Solution, since both her fa-ther and Durrfeld promoted Nazism. She dreams that her father demands her death, after not allowing her to listen to music and, as Ross suggests, her suicide "represents her final attempt to please the tyrannical parent who haunts her memory" (Ross, 11). Sophie's psychic submission, so evident in her dreams and life, obviously carries with it greater consequences, since it both is a product of and reveals support for the anti-Semitism that was rife in Poland and that went to feed the Nazi Holocaust.

Finally, both Stingo and Sophie are storytellers. Like Stingo, Sophie adores Wolfe and thinks of Faulkner as "possessed." The telling of her story leads to her death, whereas with Stingo it leads to his reconsideration of life. Both characters use language as both a shield and a probe to evade and confront their own psyches and histories in all their labyrinthine connections. It is Sophie who gives Stingo his subject, and both are darkly involved in naming the unnameable, the attraction to and repulsion for eroticism and death. Both become enmeshed in an exorcism that intermingles Eros and Thanatôs. And both in their tellings try to name the source to defuse it and in doing so exorcise the demons that haunt them. Obviously the demons of a Catholic Pole from Auschwitz and a Protestant American from the South are of a distinctly different nature, although bigotry surely plays a role in all demonology, but the two characters' attempts to exorcise the demons, whatever the cost, are remarkably similar.

After all, the older Stingo assumes Sophie's role in retelling her tale in the very manner in which she unveiled it to the younger Stingo. He relies on the same technique of revelation and concealment. Every plot ends in death of a kind. And Styron is very aware of the vampiric violation of individual souls, with all its nefarious and necessary circumstances. No one can emerge from such a process unchanged. Sophie's death gives Stingo life; her sacrifice to her demons reveals the source of knowledge about his own demons and those of his age. It is to the older Stingo that we must turn in order to try to understand the wider implications of this tunneling into the battered psyches of our age.

The Narrator: The Older Stingo

One of the first things the older Stingo, whom we shall call the narrator, does is to dissociate himself from his younger self. "In those days," as the novel begins, Stingo was twenty-two, and the nickname didn't outlive the character: "Sometime during my thirties the nickname and I mysteriously parted company, Stingo merely evaporated like a wan ghost out of my existence" (*SC*, 2). Even the name, therefore, suggests the ghost of the narrator's former self. The narrator envies Stingo's zeal as a young writer, "so long before middle age and the drowsy slack tides of inanition, gloomy boredom with fiction, and the pooping-out of ego and ambition," so driven by "immortal longings [that] impelled your every hyphen and semicolon and you had the faith of a child in the beauty you felt you were destined to bring forth" (*SC*, 133–34).

Of course such immortal longings often lack a sense of irony, and the narrator realizes this fact, thus often defusing Stingo's rhetorical effusions and espousals. "I am a little mortified to discover that almost none of the above was apparently written with the faintest trace of irony" (*SC*, 155), the narrator admits when inserting an excerpt from Stingo's journals into the narrative. And the narrator's attempt to understand in greater detail and with a wider background Sophie's story—and Stingo's—helps to place in perspective the doom-scented, gloom-haunted rhetoric.

The narrator cannot forget Sophie's tattoo; nor can he forget Sophie and Nathan "and all the interconnected and progressively worsening circumstances which led that poor straw-haired Polish darling headlong into destruction. [Such things] had preyed on my memory like a repetitive and ineradicable tic" (*SC*, 262). As Styron himself admitted in 1981, "In 1977, I had been writing a book about the Marines, 'The Way of the Warrior.' . . . I had slept well and in my dreams I had seen Sophie again, with her tattoo in the Brooklyn boarding house. I said to myself: 'Drop the Marines, she is your novel' " (Braudeau, 246). The power of that dream linked to the image of the tattoo suggests the compulsion in the narrator's need to tell his tale.

The narrator also wishes to correct Stingo's jaunty assertions. *"Someday I will understand Auschwitz,"* Stingo writes in his journal. The narrator, with his later perspective, corrects such assumptions: *"Someday I will write about Sophie's life and death, and thereby help demonstrate how absolute evil is never extinguished from the world"* (*SC*, 623). The later assertion is more modest in its scope, although it does reinforce Stingo's earlier notion that "absolute evil paralyzes absolutely" (*SC*, 479). In any case the narrator's statement leaves the ramifications of the novel more open-ended, as if frozen in place by his having looked absolute evil in the face. The exorcism is less complete, perhaps, but for that very reason much more human and ongoing.

The older Stingo, the narrator, also attempts to put 1947 in perspective, in part to lend a sense of historical accuracy to Stingo's rampaging and frustrated lust. Thus whether or not Stingo's thwarted "affair" with Leslie Lapidus touches directly on his involvement with Sophie and Nathan, it does reveal "significant things to be said about that sexually bedeviled era" (*SC*, 143). The year 1947 was "a particularly ghastly period of Eros . . . epitomized by Little Miss Cock-Tease . . . that made sex in midcentury America such a nightmarish Sargasso Sea of guilts and apprehensions" (*SC*, 145, 146). Stingo's obsessions are the obsessions of an era, buttressed by the social and personal repressions built into "the time between the puritanism of our forefathers and the arrival of public pornography" (*SC*, 145).

Stingo's sexual frustration suggests the "fabric and mood" of Styron's 1947. To Stingo his crisis of virginity in 1947 may very well have seemed like a crisis of civilization, as Frederick Karl in *American Fictions, 1940–1980* insists that it cannot be. In American terms such a crisis may have been the case and may point up once more the fortunate insulation and "luck" of being a white Anglo-Saxon Protestant in America then and not a European Jew or a Catholic Pole.

The narrator cannot help but provide a larger perspective for the narrative, particularly because of the passage of time and of his own "uncontrolled didacticism" (*SC*, 594). Thus he stops the flow of Stingo's story in order to provide explanations and interpretations from a historical perspective in much the same way that Hawthorne did in his romances. Stingo's self-absorption and trauma are placed in a wider historical perspective, one in which they gain necessary distance for interpretation and, in many cases, sympathy. The reader, not himself or herself "imprisoned" in 1947, can understand in a way that Stingo cannot what forces may have been at work upon and through him.

Therefore the narrator, for instance, describes such historical details and programs as Lebensborn and Judenrein, the systematic "cleansing" of the Jews from Poland and elsewhere to Auschwitz and Birkenau. It is he who makes explicit the social and cultural connections between Stingo's South and Sophie's Poland so as to connect them on a more openly thematic and historical level. Even the southern Gothic style seems a product of an era, part of the American romance as practiced then so eloquently by Faulkner, Carson McCullers, and others. If it alters the thing seen, as all art does and must, then it is also a historical mode within which the younger Stingo would find himself writing in any case.

Alvin Rosenfeld has charged that Styron has invented an "erotics of Auschwitz" by transferring the South's fascination with sex, death, and race—miscegenation and incest, for instance—to Poland, as if Auschwitz could then become "the erotic centerpiece of a new Southern Gothic novel."[6] In fact the "southern experience" doesn't necessarily exclude the Polish, and from an American perspective, perhaps there are distinct connections between the two.

Saul Friedlander in his provocative book *Reflections of Nazism* has described Nazi rhetoric as "one of accumulation, repetition, and redundancy. . . . [It is] the circular language of invocation, which tirelessly turns on itself and creates a kind of hypnosis by repetition, like a word that is chanted in certain prayers. . . . [It] can create . . . an impression of fusion and of sugary harmony . . . [and it] also suggests drowning, suffocation, terror, and chaos."[7] Styron is very much aware of this use of language when he describes one of Hoss's anti-Semitic tirades to Sophie "as the flow of his weird Nazi grammar, with its outlandishly overheated images and clumps of succulent Teutonic wordbloat . . . nearly drowning her reason" (*SC*, 343).

Certainly there may be similarities between Styron's rhetoric and what Friedlander classifies as "Nazi," at least in these general descriptions, but such rhetoric is not merely the prerogative of the Nazis. Styron is very aware of the seductive "evils" of language—his novel resonates with such glimpses and descriptions—but Friedlander's description and classification strikes me as simplistic and one-dimensional.

It is the narrator who wrestles with George Steiner's thesis of simultaneous time and of a sacred silence to be shared in the wake of Auschwitz. Such silence, according to Steiner, should occupy the place of any rhetorical reductionism that could lead to misunderstandings and by and large would be inadequate to the task of grappling with such an appalling mystery in any case. For the older Stingo, his reading Steiner comes as a "shock of recognition," particularly since it comes in 1967 at a moment when his own will seems paralyzed and he's experiencing the letdown after the publication of a successful novel in that year. Stingo had also experienced the notion of "some sinister metaphysical time warp" (*SC*, 267) when he realizes that on the day Sophie entered Auschwitz—April Fools' Day, 1943—he was stuffing himself with bananas to gain weight to join the marines.

The narrator can understand Steiner's celebration of silence and feels that as a narrator he is very much an intruder upon such "sacred" events but insists that "the embodiment of evil which Auschwitz has become remains impenetrable only so long as we shrink from trying to penetrate it, however inadequately." Thus he will continue to "make a stab at understanding Auschwitz by trying to understand Sophie, who to say the least was a cluster of contradictions" (*SC*, 265). As Elie Wiesel once said, "Not all victims were Jews, but all Jews were victims." Into such a labyrinthine landscape the older Stingo wishes to go.

Part of the narrator's attempts at explanation includes his siding with Simone Weil and Hannah Arendt in trying to explore the "true nature of evil" in the person of Rudolf Hoss. He decides that real evil is "gloomy, monotonous, barren, boring" and that Hoss's mind reveals the "crushingly banal" that Arendt has described evil as being (*SC*, 179). Hoss seeks refuge in duty and obedience and in his memoirs, in which he focuses on himself, the murderer, as the victim of circumstances beyond his control. His refrain of "I had to" continually indicates his "cretinous innocence" in the "moral vacuum" that is his mind (*SC*, 180). And as if to buttress this theory, the narrator points out that real evil, unlike the romanticized version in sentimental fiction, is more often committed by civilians than by the military.

The narrator also believes in the theory explored by Richard L. Rubenstein in his book *The Cunning of History*. Rubenstein suggests that

the Nazi "ethic" was based on a world of slavery, built solely on the expend-
ability of human life. Thus the Nazis produced "a new form of human society . . . of total domination, [creating] extermination center[s] to
manufacture corpses" (*SC,* 286, 288). This form of society should come as
no surprise to readers of Styron's fiction, since he has been pursuing forms
of slavery and domination as themes as early as *The Long March* and more
recently in *The Confessions of Nat Turner.*

Styron has discussed Bruno Bettelheim's theory that there are "parallels
between slavery and the concentration camp, . . . [that] in attempting to
explain why the victims of the concentration camps did not revolt, rise up,
just as . . . the slaves didn't rise up, . . . [Bettelheim is suggesting that]
they were so traumatized by their new condition that they had no opportunity [to revolt]. . . ." Bettelheim states: "The degradation of slavery and
of the concentration camps was equally and almost totally complete"
(Forkner and Schricke, 198–99). Styron, in agreeing with Bettelheim,
also views Nazism as "a new form of evil, an evil so total that it could
cause a woman to murder one of her own children. That was the central
guiding, motivating factor behind writing *Sophie's Choice*" (Lewis, 258).
Nazism, showing no Christian restraints of any kind "as it was unleashed
at Auschwitz," Styron concludes, "is of such a nature that it seems to exist
in another temporal scale; as if there were some equivalent of the 'black
holes' in space" (Barzelay and Sussman, 250).

Many critics, including Karl and Friedlander, have argued that in com-
paring Nazism to an unrestrained slave society, Styron is reducing the scope
of it. Friedlander in fact goes on to suggest that in conjuring up the mys-
tique of submission and domination, in paying obeisance to a kind of demonic mystical order of things, writers like Styron may be partaking of the
psychological forces within Nazism itself. Liberals, Friedlander maintains,
view the "totalitarian conception of Nazism . . . within the framework of
the same mechanism of domination. . . . That implies, in fact, an implicit
or explicit belief in a secret order of things determining the apparent course
of events; it is thus a matter of a complete devaluation of the order of politics" (Friedlander, 77–78). That belief suggests "that Hitler was inevitable
. . . [and that there is] a kind of empty place where there is room neither for
the rational interpretation of events nor for free and effective political action,
nor for moral and legal responsibility" (Friedlander, 78–79). And such a
perspective can lead both to man's aspiration for limitless power and his lust
for unlimited annihilation (Friedlander, 85).

Friedlander's argument is powerful. One should not lose sight of particular crimes within the larger, more generalized visions of the state of the

human soul, an idea that suggests that such particular crimes are all but inevitable. But once again, Nazism does not have exclusive rights to such visions, and in the novel Styron's views of domination and slavery, revealed in the tortured psyches of his characters, reflect the contradictory powers of such "reveries of total destruction" and the failure of politics, history, and ideologies to deal with them in some less demonic manner.

The narrator's explanation of why Dr. Jemand von Niemand forces Sophie to choose between which of her children will live and which will die raises questions about just what the older Stingo has learned in relation to his younger self. The narrator describes von Niemand's action as a religious crisis. In the absence of sin, there can be no God. Therefore, conversely, in the presence of sin, the presence of God is restored. Von Niemand forces Sophie to choose between her children by committing a monumental sin in playing God in order to restore his own belief in God. And not only the narrator but also Styron believes this to be the case, for Styron has said, "The only way of making God real in a world He has deserted is to commit the most horrible sin conceivable" (Barzelay and Sussman, 250).

Once again there are problems both with this explanation and with Styron's forthright identification with it. If *Sophie's Choice* reveals anything, it reveals mountains of available evidence to reinforce the contrary position: that notions of God, religion, and sin have become obsolete in the world the Holocaust has produced. Hoss has "broken with Christianity" (*SC*, 277) in the "cretinous innocence" within the "moral vacuum" of his mind. Why should von Niemand be any different? Von Niemand himself mocks Sophie and her Christian faith as well: "So you believe in Christ the Redeemer? . . . Did He Not say, 'Suffer the little children to come unto Me' " (*SC*, 589)? These comments precede his forcing Sophie to make her terrifying choice.

Throughout the novel, Sophie decries her loss of God or describes the monster he has become. The sampler on the wall in Emmi Hoss's room reads: "Just as the Heavenly Father saved people / from sin and from Hell, / Hitler saves the German Volk / from destruction" (*SC*, 488). In a world of total victimization and boundless cruelty, Hitler is indeed the presiding deity. Even Stingo comments about the empty rhetoric of Christianity, of how he too hates God, and how as a writer he uses scripture as "largely a literary convenience, supplying me with allusions and tag lines for the characters in my novel" (*SC*, 613). As Wanda suggests, "Despite the *Dreck* that's been written in the Gospels, adversity produces not understanding and compassion, but cruelty" (*SC*, 575). Even if Wanda goes on to suggest that there may be some sense of redemption in dying for a noble cause, the antireligious texture of the novel surely undercuts any last-minute "tag line" about sin and God's presence. It is as if the narrator—and Styron—at best has failed to understand the new world that's been produced in the novel and at worst has betrayed it.

It would seem that the presence of Auschwitz eviscerates any transcendentally Christian point of view in the novel. It would also seem that Styron and the narrator, in clinging to outworn creeds, are not reading the material clearly or are equivocating in such a manner as to ignore what has happened. Stingo's father inhabited a more or less God-fearing world in a pre-Holocaust era, but the godlessness of the post-Holocaust world seems to be the point that Sophie and the younger Stingo are making. Whispering "Jesus Christ" or "Oh God" strikes Stingo "as empty as any idiot's dream of God, or the idea that there could be such a Thing" (*SC*, 568). And if Auschwitz "effectively block[ed] the flow of that titanic love, like some fatal embolism in the bloodstream of mankind . . . or alter[ed] the nature of love entirely" (*SC*, 624), then surely von Niemand's backhand appeal to an absent God seems utterly absurd and self-deceiving.

"The book has to do with the concentration camps," Styron explained in 1974, "which in a sense is a sort of metaphysical betrayal beyond all comprehension, betrayal of the human race" (Forkner, 197). And within that betrayal must certainly lie a straightforward appeal to a religious sensibility and sentiments. Perhaps, as Michael Kreyling has suggested, Styron has fallen victim to a kind of post-Holocaust disease in which one identifies with the victims but at the same time envies the power and will of the evil manipulators.[8] Von Niemand's "religious crisis," as envisioned by the narrator, may be just one more attempt to glorify the demon, to clothe the moral banality of his dutiful obedience in robes of outmoded religious doubt and supposition.

The narrator warns us early on that "Sophie told me a number of lies that summer" (*SC*, 116). He decides that she does so in order to hold on to her sanity, evading the true horror of her prior existence in order to keep going on. Every tale embodies "a hideous sense of guilt [that] always chiefly governed the reassessments she was forced to make of her past." And because "she tended to view her own recent history through a filter of self-loathing" (*SC*, 177), her repressing the worst details helps her stay alive. As the tales are told, the guilt increases and at last overwhelms her. To complete them is to commit suicide.

But then the question remains, Why does the narrator directly imitate Sophie's repressive way of revealing her secrets? He knows the facts before he writes, of course. The truth must lie with his ultimate point of view, that of focusing on the younger Stingo's discovery of Sophie's fate and conse-

quently his loss of innocence. It also lies with the narrator's focusing on reproducing Stingo's discovery of a tragic person and theme to write about,
with revealing why Stingo became the writer he did and what needed to
happen to him in order to become that writer. The narrator's true story,
then, is Stingo's tale of self-discovery, of his shock of recognition concerning
absolute evil, the crush of history, and the horrifying realities at the heart of
the middle of the twentieth century. That recognition for the narrator is obviously more important than the fact of Sophie's death—could he really
have done anything to save her?—and the explanations of how to live in a
post-Holocaust world.

The narrator, too, may share Stingo's guilt at failing to rescue Sophie. He
is aware of his shortcomings, and because of or in spite of them Sophie has
ultimately eluded both the young and the older Stingo. After all, he has
slept with Sophie and has deserted her in the end. And the nightmares of
the dead mother sound as if they continue. His tale is the young white
male's loss of "radical innocence," a mythical American tale that resonates
throughout our literature, however limited and calculated it may be. And
perhaps those very notions of innocence taint the narrator's recollection of
his younger self and continue in altered ways to encapsulate his sense of self
within the self-encapsulating landscape Americans have come to know, and
within which they too often seek shelter.

The prerequisites for the Gothic novel or romance, the kind Styron
writes, include the sequence of withholding information, as we have discussed earlier. Such withholding increases the expectations, the suspense,
the very spell of the story as it proceeds to uncover darker and darker secrets.
The process takes on the coloring of an exorcism, that underlying psychological trajectory of the Gothic novel, whose very repressions increase the
need to confess. Such is the rhetorical foreplay, the "tunneling" effect (Karl,
537) of the Gothic novel, and without a doubt it is Styron's masterpiece in
that form.

In focusing on Stingo's shock of recognition, the development of his insight that is related to his loss of Sophie, the narrator focuses on the mythical continuities of innocence and the loss of it rather than on the radical
disruptions the presence of Auschwitz has caused in the contemporary
world. In doing so the narrator creates a fine and resonant tension between
the careful manipulations of the Gothic novel and the alien landscape its
revelations must produce at its conclusion. At one point the narrator suggests how Nathan has prefigured many of the disruptive ills of our contemporary age, but the real emphasis is the narrator's trying to fathom how that
came about. This is, after all, Stingo's book about Stingo's discoveries, and

however powerful Sophie is as a character, the novel is finally not hers. Those wishing it were are discussing a different book.

Throughout the novel both Stingos realize that the process of interpretation and understanding is also an act of penetration and violation. Often they may flinch from this knowledge, but they never relinquish it. While the younger Stingo celebrates his sexual penetration of and triumph over Sophie in his breathless, twenty-two-year-old way, he loses her. While the older Stingo grapples with the implications of Sophie's life and world, he too has lost her. The younger Stingo almost substitutes sexual release for understanding and communication, reaching "a kind of furious obsessed wordlessness finally—no Polish, no English, no language, only breath" (*SC,* 604)—and in that wordlessness celebrating sleep and death. But the older Stingo celebrates language in all its tortuous twistings and perversions as a way of trying spiritually to understand Sophie's plight, the world of the Holocaust, and his own complicitous role in it. Both cannot possess Sophie. To possess her, sexually or spiritually, is to lose her; to know is to remain empty-handed. And even the narrator realizes that "Auschwitz itself remains inexplicable" (*SC,* 623), as, ultimately, must Sophie.

And yet what Styron has accomplished in this powerful novel is that sense of recognition and complicity in which sex, death, language, and even Nazism are all inextricably bound up, not resulting in absolute paralysis and dread but revealing the psychic and powerful depths of such forces. Somewhere, Styron suggests, we are all drawn to darker designs. Somehow we are all victims and accomplices as we speak to, pursue, and use one another. That vision permeates the novel. It lies at the heart of darkness in *Sophie's Choice.* And whether or not Styron himself has recognized his own complicities in such a text, the text itself still records and reveals them all.

Sophie's Choice is a masterful, passionate vision, one filled with all the ambiguities and uncertainties that such dark visions can conjure up. The promises of *Lie Down in Darkness* are here realized, and the confessions of William Styron have reached their present fulfillment.

Notes and References

Chapter One

1. Nora Frankiel, "Styron Opens Up about His Breakdown," *Providence Journal,* 25 June 1989, H17; hereinafter cited in text.

2. Phillip Caputo, "Styron's Choices," *Esquire,* December 1986, 157; hereinafter cited in text.

3. William Styron, "Why Primo Levi Need Not Have Died," *New York Times,* 19 December 1988; hereinafter cited in text as "Levi."

4. Louis J. Slovinsky, "About Men: Out of Depression," *New York Times,* 3 January 1988, 36.

5. William Styron, "Darkness Visible," *Vanity Fair,* December 1989, 285; hereinafter cited in text as "Darkness."

6. William Styron, "A Tidewater Morning," *Esquire,* August 1987, 87, 96, 95; hereinafter cited in text as "Tidewater."

7. Michiko Kakutani, "William Styron on His Life and Work," *New York Times Book Review,* 12 December 1982, 26.

8. Glenn Collins, "Rose Styron: Catch Her if You Can," *Lears,* May 1989, 76.

9. William Styron, television interview with Dick Cavett on PBS, 1979; hereinafter cited in text as Cavett interview.

10. William Styron, interview with the author, July 1969; hereinafter cited in text as Coale.

11. Philip Rahv, "The Editor Interviews William Styron," in *Conversations with William Styron,* ed. James L.W. West III (Jackson: University Press of Mississippi, 1985), 152.

12. Editor's note, *Esquire,* August 1987, 85.

13. Michael West, "An Interview with William Styron" (6 February 1977), in *Conversations,* ed. West, 218, 219; hereinafter cited in text as M. West.

14. Douglas Brazelay and Robert Sussman, "William Styron on *The Confessions of Nat Turner:* A *Yale Lit* Interview" (1968), in *Conversations,* Ed. West, 93; hereinafter cited in text.

15. Robert K. Morris, "An Interview with William Styron," in *The Achievement of William Styron,* ed. Robert K. Morris and Irving Malin (Athens: University of Georgia Press, 1975), 33; hereinafter cited in text.

16. David S. Reynolds, *Beneath the American Renaissance* (New York: Knopf, 1988), 56.

17. Wendy McBane, "Writer Styron Recalls Days at Davidson College," *Richmond Times-Despatch,* 25 June 1988, B23.

18. Judith Ruderman, *William Styron* (New York: Ungar, 1987), 10; hereinafter cited in text.

19. Czeslaw Milosz, *The Captive Mind* (New York: Vintage Books, 1981), 80.

20. Joyce Carol Oates, "Norman Mailer: The Teleology of the Unconscious," in *New Heaven, New Earth: The Visionary Experience in Literature* (New York: Vanguard, 1974), 200.

21. John Gardner, "A Novel of Evil" [review of *Sophie's Choice, New York Times Book Review,* 27 May 1979, 1, 16–17], in *Critical Essays on William Styron,* ed. Arthur D. Casciato and James L.W. West III (Boston: G.K. Hall, 1982), 248–49; hereinafter cited in text.

22. Norman Kelvin, "The Divided Self: William Styron's Fiction from *Lie Down in Darkness* to *The Confessions of Nat Turner,*" in *Achievement,* ed. Morris and Malin, 211, 209; hereinafter cited in text.

23. David Leverenz, *The Language of Puritan Feeling* (New Brunswick, N.J.: Rutgers University Press, 1980), 24, 25.

24. Douglas Robinson, *American Apocalypses* (Baltimore: Johns Hopkins University Press, 1985), 172; hereinafter cited in text.

25. Peter Matthiessen and George Plimpton, "The Art of Fiction V: William Styron" (1954), in *Conversations,* ed. West, 10; hereinafter cited in text.

26. Marc L. Ratner, *William Styron* (New York: Twayne, 1972), 56; hereinafter cited in text.

27. Georgann Eubanks, "William Styron: The Confessions of a Southern Writer" (May 1984), in *Conversations,* ed. West, 273–74; hereinafter cited in text.

28. William Styron, "Afterword to *The Long March,*" in *Critical Essays,* ed. Casciato and West, 70; hereinafter cited as "Afterword."

29. William Styron, "The Prevalence of Wonders," in *Critical Essays,* ed. Casciato and West, 48; hereinafter cited in text as "Prevalence."

30. James L.W. West III, "A Bibliographer's Interview with William Styron" (21 December 1974), in *Conversations,* ed. West, 204.

31. Roger Asselineau, "Following *The Long March,*" in *Critical Essays,* ed. Casciato and West, 59; hereinafter cited in text.

32. Hubert Juin, "A Visit with William Styron" (1962), in *Conversations,* ed. West, 22.

33. William Styron, in a talk at Roger Williams College, 13 January 1972; hereinafter cited in text as talk at RWC.

34. Michael Braudeau, "Why I Wrote *Sophie's Choice*" (1981), in *Conversations,* ed. West, 255; hereinafter cited in text as talk at RWC.

35. Robert K. Morris and Irving Malin, "Vision and Value: The Achievement of William Styron," in *Achievement,* ed. Morris and Malin, 14; hereinafter cited in text.

Chapter Two

1. Annie Brierre, "The Prey of the Critics" (22 March 1962), in *Conversations,* ed. West, 29.

2. Charles Monaghan, "Portrait of a Man Reading" (27 October 1968), in *Conversations,* ed. West, 111.

3. William Styron, *Sophie's Choice* (New York: Random House, 1979), 418; hereinafter cited in text as *SC.*

4. Frederick Hoffman, *The Art of Southern Fiction: A Study of Some Modern Novelists* (Carbondale: Southern Illinois University Press, 1967), 16; hereinafter cited in text.

5. Richard Gray, *The Literature of Memory: Modern Writers of the American South* (Baltimore: Johns Hopkins University Press, 1977), 35; hereinafter cited in text as R. Gray.

6. Allen Tate, "A Southern Mode of the Imagination," *Collected Essays* (Denver: Alan Swallow, 1959), 560, 563.

7. James McBride Dabbs, *Who Speaks for the South?* (New York: Funk and Wagnalls, 1964), 117.

8. C. Vann Woodward, "W.J. Cash Reconsidered," *New York Review of Books,* 4 December 1969, 34.

9. William Styron, *Lie Down in Darkness* (New York: New American Library, 1979), 69; hereinafter cited in text as *LDD.*

10. William Styron, *Set This House on Fire* (New York: Bantam, 1981), 15; hereinafter cited in text as *SHF.*

11. William Styron, *This Quiet Dust and Other Writings* (New York: Random House, 1982), 89; hereinafter cited in text as *TQD.*

12. Louis D. Rubin, Jr., "Notes on a Southern Writer in Our Time," in *Achievement,* ed. Morris and Malin, 63; hereinafter cited in text.

13. Jan B. Gordon, "Permutations of Death: A Reading of *Lie Down in Darkness,*" in *Achievement,* ed. Morris and Malin, 103; hereinafter cited in text.

14. Lewis P. Simpson, "Southern Fiction," in *Harvard Guide to Contemporary American Writing,* ed. Daniel Hoffman (Cambridge, Mass.: Belknap Press, 1979), 187.

15. Lewis P. Simpson, *The Dispossessed Garden: Pastoral and History in Southern Literature* (Baton Rouge: Louisiana State University Press, 1975), 98; hereinafter cited in text.

16. Quoted in Elizabeth M. Kerr, *William Faulkner's Gothic Domain* (Port Washington, N.Y.: Kennikat, 1979), 28; hereinafter cited in text.

17. Elizabeth MacAndrew, *The Gothic Tradition in Fiction* (New York: Columbia University Press, 1979), 12; hereinafter cited in text.

18. William Styron, "Acceptance Speech for the Howells Medal," in *Critical Essays,* ed. Casciato and West, 226.

19. Robert Dale Parker, *Faulkner and the Novelistic Imagination* (Urbana: University of Illinois Press, 1985), and Gordon Hutner, *Secrets and Sympathy: Forms of Disclosure in Hawthorne's Novels* (Athens: University of Georgia Press, 1988), 36, 169.

20. William Styron, *The Confessions of Nat Turner* (New York: Random House, 1966), 424, 428; hereinafter cited in text as *CNT*.

21. Robert Phillips, "Mask and Symbol in *Set This House on Fire*," in *Achievement,* ed. Morris and Malin, 139–40.

22. Stephen Lewis, "William Styron" (1983), in *Conversations,* ed. West, 264; hereinafter cited in text.

23. Quoted in Maurice Edgar Coindreau, *A French View of Modern American Fiction* (Columbia: University of South Carolina Press, 1971), 9; hereinafter cited in text.

24. Quoted in Patrick F. Quinn, *The French Face of Edgar Poe* (Carbondale, IL: Southern Illinois University Press, 1957), 64.

25. Charles Baudelaire to Charles-Augustin Sainte-Beuve, 26 March 1856, in Rosemary Lloyd, ed., *Selected Letters of Charles Baudelaire: The Conquest of Solitude* (Chicago: University of Chicago Press, 1986), 84.

26. For a further discussion of these issues, see Jean Alexander, *Affidavits of Genius: Edgar Allan Poe and the French Critics, 1847–1924* (Port Washington, N.Y.: Kennikat Press, 1971).

27. Jean-Paul Sartre, *Essays in Existentialism* (Secaucus, N.J.: Citadel Press, 1965), 68; hereinafter cited in text. For a further discussion of existentialism and literature, see William Barrett, *Irrational Man: A Study in Existential Philosophy* (New York: Doubleday, 1958), and *Time of Need: Forms of Imagination in the Twentieth Century* (New York: Harper and Row, 1972).

28. Quoted in David Galloway, *The Absurd Hero in American Fiction,* 2d ed., (Austin: University of Texas Press, 1981), 12; hereinafter cited in text.

29. Cushing Strout, *The Veracious Imagination* (Middletown, Conn.: Wesleyan University Press, 1981), 69.

30. Donald Pease, *Visionary Compacts* (Madison: University of Wisconsin Press, 1987), 243.

31. Russell Reising, *The Unusable Past: Theory and the Study of American Literature* (New York: Metheun, 1986), 43; hereinafter cited in text.

32. David L. Stevenson, "William Styron and the Fiction of the Fifties," in *Recent American Fiction: Some Critical Views,* ed. Joseph J. Waldmeir (Boston: Houghton Mifflin, 1963), 265–66, 273–74; hereinafter cited in text.

33. Christopher Lasch, *The Culture of Narcissism* (New York: Warner Books, 1979), 103.

34. Robert N. Bellah, Richard Madsen, William M. Sullivan, Ann Swidler, and Steven M. Tipton, *Habits of the Heart* (Berkeley: University of California Press, 1985), 6.

35. Allan Bloom, *The Closing of the American Mind* (New York: Simon and Schuster, 1987), 155–56.

36. John Kenny Crane, *The Root of All Evil* (Columbia: University of South Carolina Press, 1984), 124.

37. Anthony Winner, "Adjustment, Tragic Humanism and Italy: Styron's *Set This House on Fire*," *Critical Essays*, 131; hereinafter cited in text.

38. Jonathan Baumbach, "Paradise Lost: Styron's *Lie Down in Darkness*," in *Critical Essays*, ed. Casciato and West, 32; hereinafter cited in text.

39. Carolyn Porter, *Seeing and Being* (Middletown, Conn.: Wesleyan University Press, 1981), 20, 32.

Chapter Three

1. Robert Dale Parker, *Faulkner and the Novelistic Imagination* (Urbana: University of Illinois Press, 1985), 15; hereinafter cited in text.

2. Quoted in Frederick R. Karl, *American Fictions, 1940–1980* (New York: Harper and Row, 1983), 235; hereinafter cited in text.

3. Elizabeth Janeway, "Private Emotions Privately Felt," in *Critical Essays*, ed. Casciato and West, 23.

4. Howard Mumford Jones, "A Rich, Moving Novel Introduces a Young Writer of Great Talent," in *Critical Essays*, ed. Casciato and West, 14.

5. Harvey Briet, "Dissolution of a Family," in *Critical Essays*, ed. Casciato and West, 19.

6. Michael Davitt Bell, *The Development of American Romance* (Chicago: University of Chicago Press, 1980), 173, 176, 182.

Chapter Four

1. David Minter, *The Interpreted Design as a Structural Principle in American Prose* (New Haven, Conn.: Yale University Press, 1969).

2. William Styron, *The Long March* (New York: Random House, 1952), 125; hereinafter cited in text as *LM*.

3. Irving Malin, "The Symbolic March," in *Achievement*, ed. Morris and Malin, 126, 132–33.

Chapter Five

1. Gerald Clarke, *Capote: A Biography* (New York: Simon and Schuster, 1988), 240; hereinafter cited in text.

2. Melvin J. Friedman, "Dislocations of Setting and Word: Notes on American Fiction since 1950," in *American Fiction: Historical and Critical Essays*, ed. James Nagel (Boston: Northeastern University Press, 1977), 80.

3. Abraham Rothberg, "Styron's Appointment in Sambuco," in *Critical Essays*, ed. Casciato and Webb, 81.

Chapter Six

1. Frank Lentricchia, *After the New Criticism* (Chicago: University of Chicago Press, 1980), 54–55; hereinafter cited in text.

2. George A. Panichas, ed., *The Politics of Twentieth-Century Novelists* (New York: Hawthorn Books, 1971), xxvi, xxix.

3. Norman Mailer, *The Armies of the Night* (New York: New American Library, 1967), 284.

4. William Styron, "The Uses of History in Fiction," in *Conversations,* ed. West, 128, 132.

5. R.G. Collingwood, *The Idea of History* (London: Oxford University Press, 1966), 282.

6. Thomas Gray, "The 1831 Text of *The Confessions of Nat Turner,*" in *William Styron's Nat Turner: Ten Black Writers Respond,* ed. John Henrik Clarke (Boston: Beacon Press, 1969), 104; hereinafter cited in text as T. Gray.

7. Mike Thelwell, "Back with the Wind: Mr. Styron and the Reverend Turner," in *Ten Black Writers,* ed. Clarke, 84; hereinafter cited in text.

8. Lerone Bennett, Jr., "Nat's Last White Man," in *Ten Black Writers,* ed. Clarke, 9; hereinafter cited in text.

9. Thomas Wentworth Higginson, quoted in John Henrik Clarke, "Introduction," in *Ten Black Writers,* ed. Clarke, x.

10. Ernest Kaiser, "The Failure of William Styron," in *Ten Black Writers,* ed. Clarke, 5; hereinafter cited in text.

11. Loyle Hairston, "William Styron's Nat Turner—Rogue-Nigger," in *Ten Black Writers,* ed. Clarke, 71.

12. Eldridge Cleaver, *Soul On Ice* (New York: Dell, 1970), 149.

13. John Oliver Killens, "The Confessions of Willie Styron," in *Ten Black Writers,* ed. Clarke, 43; hereinafter cited in text.

14. Vincent Harding, "You've Taken My Nat and Gone," in *Ten Black Writers,* ed. Clarke, 30.

15. Ben Forkner and Gilbert Schricke, "An Interview with William Styron" (April 1974), in *Conversations,* ed. West, 193; hereinafter cited in text.

16. Clarke, "Introduction," in *Ten Black Writers,* ed. Clarke, vii.

17. Evan Carton, *The Rhetoric of American Romance* (Baltimore: Johns Hopkins University Press, 1985), 26.

18. Richard Pearce, *William Styron* (Minneapolis: University of Minnesota Press, 1971), 43; hereinafter cited in text.

19. Leonard Butts, *The Novels of John Gardner* (Baton Rouge: Louisiana State University Press, 1988), 97, 87.

Chapter Seven

1. Emily Miller Budick, *Fiction and Historical Consciousness: The American Romance Tradition* (New Haven, Conn.: Yale University Press, 1989).

2. Ihab Hassan, *Radical Innocence* (Princeton, N.J.: Princeton University Press, 1961), 5.

3. William Heath, "I, Stingo: The Problem of Egotism in *Sophie's Choice,*" *Southern Review* 20 (July 1984): 532, 538; hereinafter cited in text.

4. Chinua Achebe, *Providence Journal,* 19 June 1988, 18.

5. Daniel W. Ross, "Dreams and the Two Plots in Styron's *Sophie's Choice"* (unpublished article, Allentown College of St. Francis de Sales, Center Valley, Pennsylvania; to be published in *Mississippi Quarterly* as "A Family Romance: Dreams and the Unified Narrative of *Sophie's Choice"*), 12; hereinafter cited in text.

6. Alvin H. Rosenfeld, "The Holocaust according to William Styron," *Midstream* 25 (December 1979): 49.

7. Saul Friedlander, *Reflections of Nazism* (New York: Avon Books, 1984), 21, 23; hereinafter cited in text.

8. Michael Kreyling, "Speakable and Unspeakable in Styron's *Sophie's Choice,"* *Southern Review* 20 (July 1984): 546–61.

Selected Bibliography

PRIMARY SOURCES

Novels

The Confessions of Nat Turner. New York: Random House, 1967. Reprint. Toronto: Bantam Books, 1983.
Lie Down in Darkness. New York: Bobbs-Merrill, 1951. Reprint. New York: New American Library, 1978.
The Long March. New York: Random House, 1952. Reprint. New York: New American Library, 1968.
Set This House on Fire. New York: Random House, 1960. Reprint. Toronto: Bantam Books, 1981.
Sophie's Choice. New York: Random House, 1979. Reprint. Toronto: Bantam Books, 1983.

Stories

"Love Day." *Esquire,* August 1985, 94–105.
"Marriott, the Marine." *Esquire,* September 1971, 101–208.
"A Tidewater Morning." *Esquire,* August 1987, 85–96.

Essays

Darkness Visible: A Memoir of Madness. New York: Random House, 1990.
This Quiet Dust and Other Writings. New York: Random House, 1982.

SECONDARY SOURCES

Caputo, Philip. "Styron's Choice's." *Esquire,* December 1986, 136–59. An in-depth interview before and after Styron's clinical depression.
Casciato, Arthur D., and **James L.W. West III,** eds. *Critical Essays on William Styron.* Boston: G.K. Hall, 1982. The best collection of reviews and some essays on Styron's fiction, including *Sophie's Choice.*
Clarke, John Henrik, ed. *William Styron's Nat Turner: Ten Black Writers Respond.* Boston: Beacon Press, 1968. A political series of essays that may have

more to do with the year in which they were published than with the novel under discussion.

Crane, John Kenny. *The Root of All Evil: The Thematic Unity of William Styron's Fiction.* Columbia: University of South Carolina Press, 1984. An excellent, well-written overview of Styron's fiction, dealing with, among other things, Styron's use of father figures, the complex narrative structure of his novels, and Styron's notions of evil.

Friedman, Melvin J. "Dislocations of Setting and Word: Notes on American Fiction since 1950." In *American Fiction: Historical and Critical Essays,* edited by James Nagel, 79–98. Boston: Northeastern University Press, 1977. An interesting discussion of Styron as a postmodernist writer, along with Vonnegut, Roth, Hawkes, and others.

Galloway, David. *The Absurd Hero in American Fiction.* Austin: University of Texas Press, 1981. An existentialist approach to Styron's characters as tragic heroes.

Gray, Richard. *The Literature of Memory: Modern Writers of the American South.* Baltimore: Johns Hopkins University Press, 1977. An overall look at the southern renaissance in modern American fiction and at Styron as a parody of that tradition, until his breakthrough novel, *The Confessions of Nat Turner.*

Heath, William. "I, Stingo: The Problem of Egotism in *Sophie's Choice.*" *Southern Review* 20, no. 3 (July 1984): 528–45. An interesting approach to the novel that views it as an unsuccessful competition between Stingo's tale and Sophie's tales.

Karl, Frederick. *American Fictions, 1940–1980.* New York: Harper and Row, 1983. A massive look at American fiction that highlights several problems with Styron's fiction in particular but views *Sophie's Choice* as Styron's greatest work.

Kreyling, Michael. "Speakable and Unspeakable in Styron's *Sophie's Choice.*" *Southern Review* 20, no. 3 (July 1984): 546–61. A fascinating account of the relationship between sex and language in Styron's novel.

Morris, Robert K., and Irving Malin, eds. *The Achievement of William Styron.* Athens: University of Georgia Press, 1975. An excellent collection of lengthy essays on the writer's work up to and including *The Confessions of Nat Turner.*

Papers on Language and Literature 23, no. 4 (Fall 1987): 419–548. A special issue devoted to Styron's fiction and including the previously unpublished short story "Blankenship."

Pearce, Richard. *William Styron.* Minneapolis: University of Minnesota Press, 1971. A short but provocative look at Styron's fiction, particularly *The Confessions of Nat Turner.*

Ratner, Marc L. *William Styron.* Boston: Twayne, 1972. A very perceptive overview of Styron's fiction through *The Confessions of Nat Turner,* particularly in its psychological suppositions.

Ruderman, Judith. *William Styron,* New York: Ungar, 1987. The most recent and a very basic overview of Styron's career and fiction.

Simpson, Lewis P. *The Dispossessed Garden: Pastoral and History in Southern Literature.* Baton Rouge: Louisiana State University Press, 1975. A mythic approach to southern fiction, with an excellent interpretation of *The Confessions of Nat Turner* and how it differs from that tradition.

Stevenson, David L. "William Styron and the Fiction of the Fifties." In *Recent American Fiction: Some Critical Views,* edited by Joseph J. Waldemir, 265–74. Boston: Houghton Mifflin, 1963. A good introduction to Styron's early work in terms of the "asocial novel" and angst-ridden fifties.

West, James L.W., III, ed. *Conversations with William Styron.* Jackson: University Press of Mississippi, 1985. An indispensable collection of interviews with Styron from 1951 to 1984.

Index

The Author

Samuel Coale has taught American literature at Wheaton College in Massachusetts since 1968 and is the author of *Paul Theroux* (Twayne, 1987), *In Hawthorne's Shadow: American Romance from Melville to Mailer* (University Press of Kentucky, 1985), *Anthony Burgess* (Unger, 1981), and the first full-length critical study of *John Cheever* (Ungar, 1977). He has written extensively on such other writers as Walt Whitman, Jerzy Kosinski, Robert Coover, Robert Frost, and Edgar Allan Poe. In 1981 he received a National Endowment for the Humanities fellowship for college teachers and in 1976–1977 was the Fulbright-Hays Senior Lecturer in American literature at Aristotelian University in Thessaloniki, Greece. He has also written about, taught in, and lectured in Czechoslovakia, Poland, Sweden, Pakistan, India, Egypt, Israel, and Brazil. Currently he is researching and writing a large work exploring the "neutral territory" of the American romance. He lives in Providence, Rhode Island, with his wife, his son, and his dog.

The Editor

Warren French (Ph.D., University of Texas, Austin) retired from Indiana University in 1986 and is now an honorary professor associated with the Board of American Studies at the University College of Swansea, Wales. In 1985 Ohio University awarded him the Doctor of Humane Letters degree. The editor of the contemporary (1945–1975) titles in Twayne's United States Authors Series, he has contributed volumes on Jack Kerouac, Frank Norris, John Steinbeck, and J.D. Salinger. His most recent publication for Twayne is *The San Francisco Poetry Renaissance, 1955–1960.*

DATE DUE			
DEC 1 1 1995			